DATE DUE			
AUG 3 '07			

BREAD
of HEAVEN

A Treasury
of CARMELITE
Prayers and
Devotions
on the
EUCHARIST

Compiled by
Penny Hickey, O.C.D.S.

Christian Classics ✦ Notre Dame, IN

Nihil obstat: given at Harrisburg, Pennsylvania, on the 23rd day of February, 2005, by Carol L. Houghton, S.T.D., J.C.D., Censor Librorum.

Imprimatur: given at Harrisburg, Pennsylvania, on the 23rd day of February, 2005, + Kevin C. Rhoades, Bishop of Harrisburg.

Founded in 1865, Ave Maria Press is a ministry of the Indiana Province of Holy Cross.

www.christian-classics.com

ISBN-10 0-87061-239-5   ISBN-13 978-0-87061-239-8

Cover and text design by John Carson

Cover photo: Erich Lessing / Art Resource, NY

Printed and bound in the United States of America.

Library of Congress Cataloging-in-Publication Data
Hickey, Penny.
  Bread of heaven : a treasury of Carmelite prayers and devotions on the Eucharist / compiled by Penny Hickey.
       p. cm.
  Includes bibliographical references.
  ISBN-13: 978-0-87061-239-8 (pbk.)
  ISBN-10: 0-87061-239-5 (pbk.)
  1. Lord's Supper--Prayer-books and devotions--English. 2. Discalced Carmelites--Prayer-books and devotions--English. I. Hickey, Penny. II. Title.

BX2169.H53 2006
242--dc22

                                        2006010797

To Abbé Chevignard ~ June 14, 1903

It seems to me that nothing better expresses the love in God's Heart than the Eucharist: it is union, consummation, he is in us, we in him, and isn't that Heaven on Earth? Heaven in faith while awaiting the face-to-face vision we so desire.

~BLESSED ELIZABETH OF THE TRINITY
LIGHT, LOVE, LIFE: ELIZABETH OF THE TRINITY

Contents

Foreword

THE DISCIPLES ON THE WAY TO EMMAUS asked Jesus to remain with them. He answered with a gift. Through the sacrament of the Eucharist, Jesus found a way to remain *with* us. Through the sacrifice of the Mass and until the end of time, we have Jesus with us under the form of bread and wine. We have—in this way—his precious presence always with us. But in this sacrament, he also found a greater gift—a way to remain in us.

Receiving the Eucharist enables us to enter into a deep communion with Jesus. Only the saints can give us some faint inkling of this mystery—Jesus always with us and Jesus within us! Why only the saints? Because the saints are true theologians. The identification of sanctity and theology may find its best support in the writings of Saint John: "Everyone who loves is begotten by God and knows God. Whoever is without love does not know God, for God is love" (1 Jn 4:7–8).

Love of God and love of neighbor are inseparable. Love is the essence of Christian sanctity—the sanctity of the Church, the sanctity of the Christian people, the sanctity of those who have been singled out by the Church as saints, blesseds, and servants of God. Through extremely diverse times, places, and cultures, all the saints have displayed this same essential quality—love, a very great love.

The knowledge of God (theology) springs from love and is measured by love. Theology is present where love is present; it is absent where love is absent. This is why Penny Hickey, in pondering the mystery of the Eucharist, turned to the saints of Carmel. Who better than they can teach and inspire us by their thoughts on the Eucharist? Their reflections arose out of their long hours of Eucharistic adoration. Hours of prayer in the presence of the Blessed Sacrament prepared them for Mass. Their deep participation in every Mass increased their longing for prayer, particularly prayer in the presence of Jesus in the sacrament. This was the secret of their tremendous love of God and neighbor.

This is a wonderful selection of Eucharistic reflections and prayers from a wide variety of saints and others from different times and places in Carmel's history. Let us hope, then, that it will provide readers with many new insights into this unfathomable mystery. But most of all, may this work increase their love for this sacrament and leave them with the desire to spend more time in his presence.

~KIERAN KAVANAUGH, O.C.D.
member of the Washington, D.C.
Carmel of Discalced Carmelite Friars
and author of many works on
Carmelite spirituality, including:
The Way of Perfection: John of the Cross:
Doctor of Light and Love and
Teresa of Avila: Interior Castle (editor)

Acknowledgments

THERE ARE SO MANY who have assisted me with this book that it is difficult to express the depth of my gratitude. First of all, Father General Luis Arostegui Gamboa, O.C.D., has really honored me with his beautiful contribution to this little book. Father Kieran Kavanaugh, O.C.D., wrote the insightful foreword for this book despite his very busy schedule. Once again, I thank Patricia O'Callaghan for her most gracious assistance at the Carmelitana Collection at Whitefriars Hall in Washington, D.C. Father John Sullivan, O.C.D., was also very generous in allowing me to use the library at the Washington, D.C. Carmelite monastery. Father William Waltersheid patiently smoothed out my Italian translations, and my daughter, Rosemary O'Neill, assisted me with the Spanish translations. I had prayed for the "gift of tongues," but God's answer came in the form of "angels" who offered to help me with translations! Thanks go, as well, to all of the publishers and authors who so kindly allowed me to use their work.

Introduction

ELIJAH WAS FED ON MOUNT CARMEL by ravens, and perhaps it was a foreshadowing of the Eucharist down through the centuries. Carmelites have found their sustenance in the Holy Eucharist.

Carmelites root their tradition in Elijah whom they see as the likely founder of the order because of his dwelling on Mt. Carmel. Excavations on Mt. Carmel have unearthed a chapel with little cells for the hermits surrounding it. For centuries, hermits have dwelled on Mt. Carmel, contemplating the awesome mystery of their Creator.

This book includes not only the saints and blesseds of Carmel's past, but extends to Carmelites in our present day. The reader will note that a number of religious initials—OCarm, O.C.D., T.O.C., or O.C.D.S.—appear after Carmelites named in this book. The OCarms are the Ancient Order of Carmel who are friars and nuns. This branch comprised the original order.

Later on, those who were participants in the reform launched by St. Teresa of Avila and St. John of the Cross were khown as Discalced Carmelites—O.C.D. "Discalced" meant "no shoes" and referred to a return to a more rigid discipline and austerities that had characterized early Carmelite communities. We are two branches of the same family, and both branches have contemplative prayer as their charism. The nuns are mostly cloistered, while the friars have active apostolates in the world. T.O.Cs. are the Third Order Carmelies of the OCarm branch. O.C.D.S. Carmelites are members of the Third (secular or lay) Order of the Discalced Carmelites.

The nuns, friars and secular Carmelites all have the privilege of receiving Holy Communion daily at the present time. But this was not always the case. Once, the Church allowed reception of the Eucharist only on special occasions or feasts. The Carmelite rule mandated time set aside each day for contemplative prayer. Many Carmelites spend this time in front of the Blessed Sacrament; others choose to do this prayer in their cells or in other places.

One can feel the ardor of these souls and the burning love for Eucharistic Jesus and for all of his people in their holy writings. This book is an invitation for everyone to read and ponder the magnitude of this mutual love—the love of Jesus in the Eucharist for his people and their love for him.

Eucharistic Jesus is the very source of our contemplation, the object of our desires, and the eternal bond between *heaven and earth*. It is my hope that readers of this work will be drawn—as if by a magnet—to a deeper devotion and heart-to-heart talks with Christ while in the presence of the Blessed Sacrament. Allow the words on these pages to be more than words to read. Let them be meat to be chewed, savored, digested, and absorbed.

Who can resist the call of the Beloved to enter his Eucharistic Heart, to love and to be loved, to speak, to be still and listen?

"O Sacrament Most Holy, O Sacrament Divine! All praise and all thanksgiving be every moment Thine!"

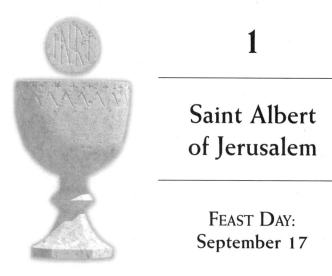

1

Saint Albert of Jerusalem

FEAST DAY:
September 17

SAINT ALBERT was born in the middle of the twelfth century in Italy. As a canon regular or religious cleric of the Holy Cross, he served as prior. Albert was made bishop of Bobbio and then of Vercelli in Italy. In 1205, he became the patriarch of Jerusalem. It was during his tenure as bishop and patriarch that he wrote the rule for the Carmelites.

The Carmelite rule of Saint Albert of Jerusalem was given to the brothers of the Most Blessed Virgin of Mount Carmel between 1206 and 1214, and approved by Pope Honorius III on January 30, 1226. Saint Albert was murdered at Acre in present day Israel in 1214.

The rule of Saint Albert of Jerusalem states: "Let an oratory be erected, as conveniently as possible, in the midst of the cells, where you are to assemble each morning to celebrate Mass when this can be conveniently done."

~*Carmelite Rule of Saint Albert*

— ✤ —

THE VERY ORIGIN of our order, therefore, includes in its rule the recommendation to attend Mass each day. In the constitution of the secular or lay Carmelite is the statement:

"We value the sacramental and liturgical life of the Church. We see it as a perennial participation in the Paschal mystery that nourishes us in our daily commitment to follow Christ crucified and risen. We participate in the celebration of the Eucharist. . . ."

~*Carmelite Secular Order Constitutions*
of Our Lady of Mount Carmel and Saint Teresa of Avila

2

Blessed
John Soreth

FEAST DAY:
July 24

BLESSED JOHN SORETH was born into an illustrious
family at Caen in Normandy about the year 1420.
Endowed with a spirit eminently adapted to great
things, and a heart full of the most heroic virtues, he
entered the Carmelite order at the age of sixteen. After
a brilliant academic career at the University of Paris, he
received the degree of Doctor of Theology in 1441. He
became prior-general or superior general for the
Carmelites in 1451. He constantly refused the office of
bishop and the cardinal's hat which Pope Calixtus III
wished to bestow upon him.

For twenty years, John labored to reform and build
his order. He canonically erected the first monastery for
Carmelite nuns in Europe. The nuns had long been a
presence in the order, particularly in the East. Later, he
founded five other convents which he guided with the

most paternal care. He gave the holy habit to Blessed Frances of Amboise, Duchess of Brittany, one of Carmel's most illustrious saints.

Several popes honored Blessed John with their confidence, and so great were his poverty, penance, and humility that he was called "the light of all the Mendicant Orders." In his zeal for the spread of the Carmelite order, he traveled throughout Europe enduring indescribable trials.

At the siege of Liège in France, sacrilegious men tore the ciborium from the altar and impiously trampled the Eucharist underfoot. Unable to endure this outrage, Blessed John forced his way into the church through crowds of enraged men. Bravely exposing his body to attack, John reverently collected the sacred hosts and carried them back to his own monastery.

Seized with a sudden illness, he received the last sacraments of the Church and exhorted his religious brothers and sisters to live in harmony and observance of the rule. He died, breathing forth his favorite aspiration, "Jesus, be to me Jesus!"

~PRAYER CARD
CARMELITE NUNS OF WHEELING, WEST VIRGINIA

— ✤ —

The rule of Blessed John Soreth states: "An oratory should be conveniently constructed in the middle of the cells." He continued the Rule of Saint Albert in encouraging daily Mass.

3

Saint Teresa
of Avila
Doctor of the Church

FEAST DAY:
October 15

TERESA DE CEPEDA Y AHUMADA was born in Avila, Spain in 1515. She was a dauntless person of zeal from a very young age. As children, she and her brother were actually going to run away to Africa to become martyrs for Christ.

As she grew older, however, Teresa became more and more enamored with pretty clothes and socializing. She gradually tamed these inclinations somewhat and entered Carmel in 1535. Saint Teresa is best known as the reformer of the order. The Carmel or Carmelite house she joined was overcrowded with nearly one hundred nuns living in it. Some of the nuns had come from very wealthy or titled families, and they used this to their advantage within the convent.

There were many social visits in the parlor, and these things seemed to draw nuns away from their charism of prayer. Teresa saw that the nuns would profit much more by returning to the original Carmelite way of life. This realization motivated her reform, which began in 1562. Traveling all over Spain and enduring great hardships and opposition, she established sixteen foundations, or reformed houses, during her lifetime.

Teresa is also known as a stalwart patron of prayer. She insisted on it for her nuns and thrived on it herself. Her love for Jesus in the Blessed Sacrament would break forth in ardent prayer and ecstasies. When each of her houses was begun, the immediate priority was to reserve the Blessed Sacrament and have Mass celebrated.

It was during one of Teresa's post-Communion prayers that she experienced the spiritual betrothal and marriage to Jesus. She was given wonderful insights into the Blessed Trinity and other mystical gifts. On one occasion, she was kneeling and preparing to receive Holy Communion. She realized that she was going to be raised in levitation and asked nuns nearby to hold her down so that the others would not notice. This was to no avail. Teresa rose in ecstacy with the visions she had of heaven.

As much as Saint Teresa revered this holy sacrament, she had to warn her nuns with these words: "Since in receiving Holy Communion we, for the most part, experience tenderness and delight, that desire to receive again was taking hold of me. If its purpose was to have God within my soul, I already had him; if it was to fulfill the obligation of going to Holy Communion, I had already done so; if to receive the favors that are bestowed with the Blessed Sacrament, I had already received them," she wrote in *The Foundations*. "Finally, I came to understand clearly that there was no other purpose in the desire than to experience the sensible delight."

When she was dying, it is reported that she seemed younger in appearance and healthier . . . actually radiant after receiving Holy Communion. She died in 1582. This dear Doctor of the Church left many of her writings for us to get a glimpse of her love and devotion for the Blessed Sacrament.

~*THE FOUNDATIONS, TERESA OF AVILA*, P. 131

— ✤ —

O MY LORD AND MY GOD! I cannot say this without tears and great joy of soul! How you desire, Lord, thus to be with us and to be present in the sacrament (for in all truth this can be believed since it is so, and in the fullness of truth we can make this comparison); and if it were not for our fault we could rejoice in being with you, and you would be glad to be with us since you say that your delight is to be with the children of the earth. O my Lord! What is this? As often as I hear these words, they bring me great consolation; they did so even when I was far gone. . . .

~*THE BOOK OF HER LIFE*, TERESA OF AVILA, P. 138

SPEAKING OF THE THIRD WATER OF PRAYER, irrigation, Teresa reveals to her confessor: The Lord today after Communion granted me this prayer; and interrupting my thanksgiving, he put before me these comparisons, taught me the manner of explaining it, and what the soul must do here. Certainly I was startled and I understood at once. Often I had been as though bewildered and inebriated by this love, and never was I able to understand its nature. I understood clearly that it was God's work, but I couldn't understand how he was working in this stage. For the truth of the matter is that the faculties are almost totally united with God but not so absorbed as not to function. I am extremely pleased that I now understand it. Blessed be the Lord who so favored me!

~*THE BOOK OF HER LIFE*, TERESA OF AVILA, P. 148

NOT SINCE THIS MORNING when I received Communion do I think it is I who am speaking. It seems that what I see is a dream, and I would desire to see no other persons than those who are sick with this sickness I now have. I beg your reverence that we may all be mad for love of him who for love of us was called man.

~*THE BOOK OF HER LIFE*, TERESA OF AVILA, P. 150

AFTER HAVING RECEIVED COMMUNION and been in this very prayer I'm writing about, I was thinking when I wanted to write something on it of what the soul did during that time. The Lord spoke these words to me: "It detaches itself from everything, daughter, so as to abide more in me. It is no longer the soul that lives but I. Since it cannot comprehend what it understands, there is an understanding by not understanding."

~*THE BOOK OF HER LIFE,* TERESA OF AVILA, P. 163

I HAD BEEN DEVOTED all my life to Christ. . . and I always returned to my custom of rejoicing in this Lord, especially when I received Communion.

~*THE BOOK OF HER LIFE,* TERESA OF AVILA, P. 192

WE HAVE HIM SO NEAR IN THE BLESSED SACRAMENT, where he is already glorified and where we don't have to gaze upon him as being so tired and worn out, bleeding, wearied by his journeys, persecuted by those for whom he did so much good, and not believed in by the Apostles. . . . Behold him here without suffering, full of glory, before ascending into heaven, strengthening some, encouraging others, our companion in the most Blessed Sacrament.

~*THE BOOK OF HER LIFE,* TERESA OF AVILA, P. 193

SOMETIMES HE COMES WITH SUCH GREAT MAJESTY that no one could doubt but that it is the Lord himself.

Especially after receiving Holy Communion—for we know that he is present since our faith tells us this—he reveals himself as so much the Lord of this dwelling that it seems the soul is completely dissolved; and sees itself consumed in Christ. O my Jesus! Who could make known the majesty with which you reveal yourself!

~*THE BOOK OF HER LIFE,* TERESA OF AVILA, P. 240

THE LORD ALMOST ALWAYS SHOWED HIMSELF TO ME as risen, also when he appeared in the host—except at times when he showed me his wounds in order to encourage me when I was suffering tribulation.

~*THE BOOK OF HER LIFE,* TERESA OF AVILA, P. 247

SOMETIMES (OR ALMOST ORDINARILY—AT LEAST, quite often) after receiving Holy Communion I was at peace. And sometimes in approaching the sacrament I felt at once so good in soul and body that I was surprised.

~*THE BOOK OF HER LIFE,* TERESA OF AVILA, P. 260

ONE DAY AFTER COMMUNION, His Majesty earnestly commanded me to strive for this new monastery with all my powers, and he made great promises that it would be founded and that he would be highly served in it.

~*THE BOOK OF LIFE,* TERESA OF AVILA, P. 280

WHEN SAINT TERESA was trying to make a foundation and lacked the means to do so, our Lord told her one day after Communion: "I've already told you to enter as best you can." And then he added: "O covetousness of the human race, that you think you will be lacking even ground!"

~*The Book of Her Life,* Teresa of Avila, p. 290

Well, with me it was like being in glory to see the Blessed Sacrament reserved.

~*The Book of Life,* Teresa of Avila, p. 311

The devil by chance may have intended to take away my peace and quiet so that on account of such disturbances I wouldn't be able to pray and thus would lose my soul. Finding myself in such a condition, I made a visit to the Blessed Sacrament, although I couldn't pray.

~*The Book of Her Life,* Teresa of Avila, p. 313

O wealth of the poor, how admirably you know how to sustain souls! And without their seeing such great wealth, you show it to them little by little. When I behold majesty as extraordinary as this concealed in something as small as the host, it happens afterward that I marvel at wisdom so wonderful, and I fail to know how the Lord gives me the courage or strength to approach him. If he who has granted, and still does grant me so many favors, did not give this strength, it would be impossible to conceal the fact or resist shouting aloud about marvels so great. For what will a wretched person, like myself, who is weighed down with abominations and who has wasted her life with so little fear of God, feel when she sees she is approaching this Lord of such powerful majesty and that this Lord desires that the soul behold it? How will a mouth that has spoken so many words against this very Lord be united with that most glorious body, which abounds in purity and compassion?

~*The Book of Life*, Teresa of Avila, pp. 337, 338

"On occasion there came over me such ardent desires to receive Communion that I don't think they could be exaggerated. They came upon me one morning when it was raining so hard it seemed impossible to leave the house. When I was outside the house, I was already so outside myself with the desire for Communion that even should lances have been held to my heart I think I'd have gone into their midst; how much more into the midst of rain." Then Teresa was caught up in a rapture where she saw a throne with animals supporting it. She saw a multitude of angels more beautiful than she had seen in heaven. She remained in that rapture and glory for two hours! Then she relates:

"I was present at Mass and received Communion, but I don't know how it was possible. It seemed to me only a short time had passed."

~*The Book of Life*, Teresa of Avila, pp. 351, 352

I HAVE EXPERIENCED FOR MORE THAN A HALF YEAR that at least when I am receiving Communion I noticeably and clearly feel bodily health. Sometimes I feel this by means of raptures, which occasionally last more than three hours. At other times I am greatly improved throughout the whole day.

~*THE BOOK OF LIFE*, TERESA OF AVILA, P. 378

ONE DAY AFTER RECEIVING COMMUNION, it seemed most clear to me that our Lord sat beside me; and he began to console me with great favors, and he told me among other things: "See me here daughter, for it is I; give me your hands." And it seemed he took them and placed them on his side and said: "Behold my wounds. You are not without me. This short life is passing away." From certain things he told me, I understood that after he ascended to heaven, he never came down to earth to commune with anyone except in the most Blessed Sacrament.

~*THE BOOK OF LIFE*, TERESA OF AVILA, P. 390

ON THE TUESDAY FOLLOWING ASCENSION THURSDAY, having remained a while in prayer after Communion, I was grieved because I was so distracted I couldn't concentrate. So I complained to the Lord about our miserable nature. My soul began to enkindle, and it seemed to me I knew clearly, in an intellectual vision, that the entire Blessed Trinity was present.

~*THE BOOK OF HER LIFE*, TERESA OF AVILA, P. 391

ONCE, A LITTLE BEFORE THIS, when I was about to receive Communion, and the host was still in the ciborium—for it hadn't been given to me yet—I saw a kind of dove that was noisily fluttering its wings. It alarmed me and caused suspension of my faculties that much effort was required to receive the host. This all happened at Saint Joseph's in Avila. Father Francisco de Salcedo gave me the Blessed Sacrament.

On another day, while hearing his Mass, I saw the Lord glorified in the host. He told me that Father Francisco's sacrifice was pleasing to him.

~*THE BOOK OF LIFE,* TERESA OF AVILA, P. 392

ON PALM SUNDAY AFTER COMMUNION, my faculties remained in such deep suspension that I couldn't even swallow the host; and, holding it in my mouth, after I returned a little to myself, it truly seemed to me that my entire mouth was filled with blood. I felt that my face and all the rest of me also was covered with it. It seemed to me warm, and the sweetness I then experienced was extraordinary. The Lord said to me: "Daughter, I want my blood to be beneficial to you, and don't be afraid that my mercy will fail you. I shed it with many sufferings, and you enjoy it with the great delight you are aware of; I repay you well for the banquet you prepare me this day."

~*THE BOOK OF HER LIFE,* TERESA OF AVILA, P. 396

While at the Incarnation [convent] in the second year that I was prioress, on the octave of the feast of Saint Martin, when I was receiving Communion, Father John of the Cross who was giving me the Blessed Sacrament broke the host to provide for another sister. I thought there was no lack of hosts but that he wanted to mortify me because I had told him it pleased me very much when the hosts were large (not that I didn't understand that the size made no difference with regard to the Lord's being wholly present, even when the particle is very small). His Majesty said to me: "Don't fear, daughter, for no one will be a party to separating you from me," making me thereby understand that what just happened didn't matter. Then he appeared to me in an imaginative vision, as at other times, very interiorly, and he gave me his right hand and said: "Behold this nail; it is a sign you will be my bride from today on. Until now you have not merited this, from now on not only will you look after my honor as being the honor of your creator, king, and God, but you will look after it as my true bride. My honor is yours, and yours mine."

~*The Book of Her Life,* Teresa of Avila, p. 402

Once after receiving Communion, I was given understanding of how the Father receives within our soul the most holy Body of Christ, and of how I know and have seen that these Divine Persons are present, and of how pleasing to the Father this offering of his son is, because he delights and rejoices with him here—let us say—on earth. Thus the humanity is so welcome and pleasing to the Father who bestows on us so many favors. I understood that he also receives this sacrifice from the priest who is in sin, except that he doesn't grant to his soul the favors he grants to those who are in the state of grace.

There are deep secrets revealed when one receives Communion. It is a pity that these bodies of ours do not let us enjoy them.

~*THE BOOK OF HER LIFE,* TERESA OF AVILA, PP. 414, 415

IN SAINT TERESA'S MEDITATION on *The Lord's Prayer,* she says in regard to the Blessed Sacrament: He asks again for no more than to be with us this day only, because it is a fact that he has given us this most sacred bread forever. His Majesty gave us, as I have said, the manna and nourishment of his humanity, that we might find him at will and not die of hunger, save through our own fault. In no matter how many ways the soul may desire to eat, it will find delight and consolation in the most Blessed Sacrament. He is teaching us to set our wills on heavenly things and to ask that we might begin enjoying him from here below; and would he get us involved in something so base as asking to eat? As if he didn't know us!

There is no need or trial or persecution that is not easy to suffer if we begin to enjoy the delight and consolation of this sacred bread.

~*THE WAY OF PERFECTION,* TERESA OF AVILA, P. 169

Do you think this heavenly food fails to provide sustenance, even for these bodies, that it is not a great medicine even for bodily ills? I know that it is. I know a person with serious illnesses, who often experiences great pain, who through this bread had them taken away as though by a gesture of the hand and was made completely well.

But the Lord had given her such a living faith that when she heard some persons saying they would have liked to have lived at the time Christ our God walked in the world, she used to laugh to herself. She wondered what more they wanted since in the most Blessed Sacrament they had him just as truly present as he was then.

~*The Way of Perfection,* Teresa of Avila, p. 171

Receiving Communion is not like picturing with the imagination, as when we reflect upon the Lord on the cross or in other episodes of the Passion, when we picture within ourselves how things happened to him in the past. In Communion, the event is happening now, and it is entirely true.

Since we know that Jesus is with us as long as the natural heat doesn't consume the accidents of bread, we should approach him. Now, then, if when he went about in the world the mere touch of his robes cured the sick, why doubt, if we have faith, that miracles will be worked while He is within us and that he will give what we ask of him since he is in our house? His

Majesty is not accustomed to paying poorly for his lodging if the hospitality is good.

~*THE WAY OF PERFECTION*, TERESA OF AVILA, P. 172

BE WITH HIM WILLINGLY; don't lose so good an occasion for conversing with him as is the hour after having received Communion. If obedience should command something, Sisters, strive to leave your soul with the Lord. If you immediately turn your thoughts to other things, if you pay no attention, and take no account of the fact that he is within you, how will he be able to reveal himself to you? This, then, is a good time for our Master to teach us, and for us to listen to him, kiss his feet because he wanted to teach us, and beg him not to leave.

~*THE WAY OF PERFECTION*, TERESA OF AVILA, P. 173

BUT AFTER HAVING RECEIVED THE LORD, since you have the person himself present, strive to close the eyes of the body and open those of the soul and look into your own heart.

~*THE WAY OF PERFECTION*, TERESA OF AVILA, P. 173

SO HIS MAJESTY IS BEING MERCIFUL ENOUGH to all of us who love him, by letting us know that it is he who is present in the most Blessed Sacrament. He doesn't want to show himself openly, communicate his grandeurs, and give his treasures except to those who he knows desire him greatly; these are his true friends.

~*The Way of Perfection*, Teresa of Avila, p. 174

CERTAINLY, I THINK that if we were to approach the most Blessed Sacrament with great faith and love, once would be enough to leave us rich. How much richer from approaching so many times as we do. The trouble is we do so out of routine, and it shows. O miserable world, you have so covered the eyes of those who live in you that they do not see the treasures by which they could win everlasting riches!

~*The Way of Perfection*, Teresa of Avila, p. 241

4

Saint John
of the Cross
Doctor of the Church

FEAST DAY:
December 14

SAINT JOHN OF THE CROSS (Juan de Yepes), extraordinary poet and spiritual guide to many, was born in Fontiveros, Spain, in 1542. He is known to have been artistic, musical, gentle, and was a great mystic. Among his great works are *The Spiritual Canticle, The Dark Night of the Soul, The Ascent of Mount Carmel,* and *The Living Flame of Love.* Meeting Saint Teresa of Avila right after his ordination was a blessing that produced fruit down through the centuries. He introduced the Carmelite reform to the friars, but met with such opposition from them that he was jailed in a monastery for several months. Eventually, he escaped and continued the reform. He died in very humble surroundings in a monastery where he was not popular in 1591. The blessing of a humble death had been his fervent desire.

Saint John of the Cross did not write explicitly about the Eucharist as did Saint Teresa. This does not mean, however, that he did not have the same devotion or a greater one. He just didn't write of it. We know that John loved to spend long hours in front of the Blessed Sacrament in the monastery at Salamanca in Spain. On arriving at a monastery, he always made it a point to greet the sick right after his visit to the Blessed Sacrament. Requiring little sleep, he spent much of the night in prayer, sometimes kneeling at the altar steps before the Blessed Sacrament. . . .

Witnesses of his life spoke of the devotion with which he celebrated Mass. A center of his contemplation, Mass often proved to be an occasion for special graces. During the celebration, he could become so lost in God that he had no consciousness of his surroundings. His greatest suffering during the imprisonment in Toledo was being deprived of the Eucharist. The Blessed Sacrament was "all his glory, all his happiness, and for him far surpassed all the things of the earth." The one privilege he accepted when he was major superior in Segovia was having the cell closest to the Blessed Sacrament.

~*INTRODUCTION TO THE WORKS OF SAINT JOHN OF THE CROSS*

— ✤ —

When Saint John was dying, he asked for the Blessed Sacrament to be brought to his cell for adoration. Once the Eucharist was brought to his cell, he poured himself out in tender devotion to the Lord, edifying and touching those present. In bidding his farewell, he said: "Now, Lord, I will not have to see you again with mortal eyes." He died a short time later.

~Life, Times and Teaching of St. John of the Cross, p. 369

5

Saint Mary Magdalen de' Pazzi

Feast Day:
May 25

CATERINA DE' PAZZI was born in 1566, in Florence, Italy, to a family of nobility, but her family's wealth and position did not attract her. Instead, she was led to service in charity and to a life of penance. Caterina made her First Communion at the age of ten, and a little later vowed herself to God as a virgin. She had an intense love for the Blessed Sacrament, and she actually delighted in touching and being near to those who were speaking of it or who had just been to Communion. She chose the Carmelite order because of the rule of receiving Communion daily.

She was a very gifted Carmelite nun who had many ecstasies, raptures, and other mystical graces including spiritual marriage. The words that she spoke during her ecstasies have been recorded in seven volumes. Saint Mary Magdalen died in 1607, and her incorrupt body lies in the Carmel in Florence. She was canonized in 1669.

— ✤ —

Teaching on Most Holy Communion

1. When you are to receive Communion, think that you are about to perform the greatest and most worthy action that can be done, which is to receive the Lord God within yourself.
2. Guard against going to Communion through habit or by chance; but go with actual devotion.
3. If you realized that as long as the sacramental species continue, you have within you the entire Most Holy Trinity, you would not go to Communion only occasionally; and you would also think about it before you left off Communion, in order not to be deprived of so great a good.
4. Take care lest, on account of your little desire and disposition, you may be the cause of closing that little window of heaven.
5. One cannot find a more effective means of perfecting a soul than to approach this divine table; and if you knew how to use this well, in a short time you

would become filled with the love of God, for only one Communion is enough to make a soul holy.

6. Never of your own will deprive yourself of Communion, because you do not know if that Communion might be the very time when God has determined to give you some grace and particular gift.

~COMPLETE WORKS OF SAINT MARY MAGDALEN DÉ PAZZI,
VOLUME 1, P. 263

SAINT MARY MAGDALEN would often say, when she saw some neglecting to receive the Most Holy Sacrament of the altar: "O Sisters, if you could be worthy, even in the least degree, of the great thing of which you have deprived yourselves this morning by not receiving Communion, you would do nothing else today but weep. For in receiving God in the most holy Sacrament, you receive the entire Most Holy Trinity for as long as those accidents of the most sacred Host remain within you; during all that time, I say, those eternal and admirable operations that are continually going on among those Divine Persons go on within yourselves." Hence, with admirable feeling, she said: "Oh, what an honor this is for a creature! But it is not known and still less realized."

~COMPLETE WORKS OF SAINT MARY MAGDALEN DÉ PAZZI,
VOLUME 1, P. 313

JUST FOR THE SAKE of daily reception of Holy Communion, she chose the monastery of Santa Maria degli Angeli. As the divine love grew in her, she came to think it impossible to live without daily Communion. She never voluntarily omitted it. Even in her illness she tried not to be left without it as far as possible. One day during her novitiate, it happened that the father confessor delayed the hour of Communion unusually, so that the mistress of novices, thinking he was no longer coming, obliged Magdalen to [eat] breakfast. No sooner did she, against her will and by mere obedience, swallow a mouthful than the father arrived and had the bell rung for Communion. The holy novice felt such regret and grief at this, and broke into such bitter weeping, as to make the mistress, who had been the cause of her disciple's being deprived of so much good that morning, weep also.

The saint was so transported by the wish of uniting herself with Jesus by means of this divine sacrament, that even the interval between one day and the other was very painful for her; and at the time of Communion it often happened that while impatiently waiting for her turn in the order of seniority, without thinking, she would go ahead of the others, sometimes even the very superioress. The fervor and reverence with which she approached the Sacred Banquet a man could scarcely imagine. It can well be said, that strengthened and kindled in the love of God by thus nourishing herself with it, she was continually in her thoughts, discourses, and most ardent desires sitting at the Celestial Banquet, so that, as a rule, before or after Communion, she was alienated from her senses.

Reflecting either on the love shown us by Jesus in the Eucharist, or on his Passion in memory of which this was instituted, she would first become inflamed with the most loving gratitude, and then, beginning to consider her nothingness in comparison to the infinite divine greatness she would approach to receive this sacrament with so profound a reverence and fear that she used to say she was expecting, some time, on account of her unworthiness, that the earth would open under her feet in the performance of this action.

She even became ecstatic in her preparation for Holy Communion and would receive it in that state. One morning the bell rang for Holy Communion and she was making bread. She had been carried out of her senses and went to Holy Communion forgetting that she still had flour on her hands and her arms were bare. She could even hear the bell summoning them to Communion when it seemed impossible to do so because of the distance. Sometimes she felt a reluctance to receive so great a gift and would say: "Oh, how great a thing it is to receive a God!"

Before the Blessed Sacrament, she seemed angelic; and when the confessor exposed it for adoration, her eyes sparkled for joy, and in her voice and the movements of her body she manifested the excess of her contentment. Her devotion to Christ was so great that during the day she would visit him thirty times, according to the order she had received from Jesus himself in the rules she mentioned. She used to call Thursday "the day of love," on account of the institution of the Eucharist which took place on that day; and she felt a special desire that the sisters would receive Communion on that day.

~THE LIFE OF SAINT MARY MAGDALEN DE-PAZZI, P. 171

DURING HER ECSTASIES, she had most sublime revelations concerning this great gift of God. In one of them, the eternal Father taught her the manner of preparing for Holy Communion. In another ecstasy, she spoke wonderfully of how the Incarnate Word rests himself in the soul and in the Church. Because of her great desire for him, she said that Jesus often would give himself to her in his own hands. She said: "My Beloved, white and ruddy, placed himself in my soul."

On the feast of Saint Albert the Carmelite, the confessor was unable to come, and the nuns had all gathered in the Communion room and Magdalen went into ecstasy. When she returned to her senses, she related that Saint Albert himself had come and distributed Holy Communion to her and all the other nuns.

~THE LIFE OF SAINT MARY MAGDALEN DE-PAZZI, P. 172

THIS AMAZING SAINT was also privileged to see Jesus in the hearts of the sisters after they had received Holy Communion. He manifested himself in some as a child, in others at the age of thirty-three, in others as suffering and crucified, and in others as risen and glorious.

~ *The Life of Saint Mary Magdalen De-Pazzi*, p. 172

At another time she uttered: "Oh! What love do I feel for all these sisters, seeing them all like so many tabernacles and ciboriums of the Most Holy Sacrament they so often receive!"

Mary Magdalen was exhorting the sisters concerning frequent reception of Holy Communion and praying of the *Consummatuum est* ["It is finished," the final words of Jesus]. She said that in this heavenly food there is contained all good, therefore what more could the soul desire? If one desires perfect charity . . . He is there. If another wishes humility, or hope, or meekness, purity . . . He is there with his virtues. "All are gathered in that wonderful God who is truly present in that Sacrament and also sitting in the hand of his Father in Heaven. Ah! How well then the soul, having and professing this God, can say with truth: '*consummatum est!*' She wants for nothing, she wishes for nothing, she longs for nothing else but him who then has given himself wholly to her, communicating to her, together all of his goods."

The saint recommended that the nuns spend time from the reception of Holy Communion to Vespers, [the evening prayer] in thanksgiving for their Holy Communion. From Vespers to the next reception of Holy Communion was to be spent in preparation by thinking of the One who was to be received and who they were before God. She regretted it when nuns would quickly rush to their duties after receiving our Lord, and told them that they were missing a wonderful time to be present to our Lord who was within them.

~*THE LIFE OF SAINT MARY MAGDALEN DE-PAZZI*, P. 175

6

Blessed Mary of the Angels

MARIANNA FONTANELLA was born in 1661 at Baldinero, Italy. There were twelve children in her family. At a very young age, she was drawn to the Eucharist. She begged her mother and her confessor to allow her to make her first Communion, but she was deemed to be too young.

She tells her story this way: "On the feast of Our Lady of the Snows, I felt an inspiration to go to the church of Saint Roch. I dared not mention it to my mother, fearing a refusal; but when I found I could have no peace on account of the interior instinct which urged me, I expressed my desire, and she acceded to it. I then set off with one of my brothers; I entered the church and observed a great many persons receiving Holy Communion. A strong desire of receiving seized me, but not having permission, I began to sigh and burst into tears. In this disposition I went to kneel at the feet of a priest [who was dressed] in a religious habit [and] who was hearing confessions.

"I continued to weep, and so vehemently that for some time I could not utter one word. He asked me why I sobbed so. I answered that my confessor was constantly postponing the time of my first Communion, adding that he knew me to be vain, worthless, and wicked, and so put me off rightly. The good religious then asked me if I wished to continue to make my confessions to himself. On my answering in the affirmative, he said: 'Go then, my child, and with an ardent desire of communicating, open and shut your mouth each time you see others going to Communion, and I promise you Our Lord will enter your heart.' I followed his advice, and it brought me such contentment and consolation that I was delighted. I remained in church until the noon-day Angelus, wholly absorbed in God, forgetting home and the world."

Eventually, she tasted such sweets in spiritual Communions that her parents had often to awaken her out of her rapture of love. . . . At last her confessor permitted her to begin a novena, preparatory to making her first Communion. She described this novena in these words: "I was weeping." She made her first Communion on the feast of the Assumption of Our Lady into heaven.

At the age of twelve, she entered the Cistercians, but had to depart to care for her family upon her father's death. Four years later, she entered the Carmelites in Turin where she was to become novice mistress, and prioress. Mary of the Angels died December 16, 1717, and was beatified in 1865.

~*BLESSED MARY OF THE ANGELS*, PP. 9, 10

7

Venerable Mother
Thérèse of
Saint Augustine

PRINCESS LOUISE MARIE was the daughter of King Louis XV and Queen Maria Leczinska of France and was born in 1737. She miraculously survived two accidents and was convinced that she owed these blessings to Our Lady's intervention. Later, she gave up the luxuries and privileges of her French royal family to be wed to Jesus, the King of Kings at the Carmelite monastery of Saint-Denis, France.

During her time at the convent, Thérèse of Saint Augustine used her influence for the cause of religion. She set a wonderful example for the other nuns by kneeling at prayer even though it was very difficult with the leg injury she had received during her childhood accident. She died in 1787, probably from poisoning. Enemies of her father, the king, had decided to end her positive influence over him and his court.

Venerable Thérèse had a deep devotion to the Eucharist which is manifested in her journal, *Meditations Eucharistiques.*

— ✣ —

Exercise

FOR THE FEAST OF THE PRESENTATION of the Holy Virgin, the anniversary day of my First Communion.

How glorious and favorable for me, [is] this day that the Church dedicates to celebrating the first offering that Mary made of herself to our Lord her God! One of the first favors was that he elevated me to the dignity of his child in baptism. He added to that by giving himself more intimately to me in communion, in the gift of his body and his blood. O what a favor! . . . I will not be able to recall the privileges with enough gratitude.

How can I better respond than by imitating in each of my Communions, the love of Mary for Jesus? An attentive love, a generous love, a faithful love. That's what she gave him. These are the same sentiments which must animate me each time I have the happiness of being united with Jesus Christ in the reception of the Eucharist.

The spirit of knowledge Mary possessed was pure from the first instant of her conception. From then on, her reason developed. For this reason, we can see what a noble mind was shaped in the little Mary as she gradually devoted herself to the Master whom she served. What ardor burned in the heart of the young Mary who was presented to God in the temple as a very young child. The tender affections of Anne and Joachim were not an obstacle to her pious sentiments. As she grew older, Mary desired to be completely for the Lord.

Such, by the grace of God, was the way I felt in my First Communion. Could I ever forget that I could never better attract the love of Jesus in the Eucharist than by fervently preparing for my first Communion? What precious, what abundant treasures slowly gathered in Mary's heart, enriching it with a new lustre? She was to become the living abode of the Holy of Holies.

Saint Ambrose paints for me an edifying image of Mary. What modesty, says this holy Father, shines on her forehead. What humility in her constancy! What harmony in the most profound meditations in her spirit. She announces and appears before the altar of the Eternal as the most holy of his creatures. When she was of age, she publicly consecrated herself and put no limit on the generosity of love which inspired her.

Her beloved, God, is all for her, and she promised to be all for her beloved. From then on, she would not envy the most flattering prerogatives of the world. The hiddenness and the solitude of the temple was to keep her happy. No earthly brilliance would touch her. With the true light of grace, she would be placed forever in the middle of darkness. She was far from regretting her loss of ease and privileges. What worldly rewards could capture the attention and ambitions of Mary while she possessed the altar of all good?

A mortified life and suffering would come to her. She had contracted for them on this day, the day on which her life and love was presented to the Father. She could not ignore him, of course, as he gradually enlightened her of the mysteries to come. But his generous love softened in advance all the rigorous sacrifices which he had reserved for her. God made invisible to her eyes the sadness which would one day pierce her soul.

I am animated by this model from Mary. Her spirit must also mark my own piety. In each Communion, I must offer to Jesus Christ a heart destined and determined to refuse him nothing. Inside of me, I still find vanity, laziness, thoughtlessness, dissipation, a taste for trifles, sensuousness, greed, an incertitude in my resolution to live out certain virtues. The generosity of my love must be disposed to destroy, to sacrifice, or at least to combat these weaknesses. Yes, this is an indispensable law for my courage. My union with Jesus, the victim on the altar, imposes these constraints on me.

I will obey with his grace. If a spiritual ardor hastened to lead the young Mary to the temple, if a most perfect generosity directed her sacrifice, and if a most faithful love crowned all her holy dispositions, then I too can make holy resolutions.

In commiting myself to follow the virtues which characterized all of her days, even from her first education in the temple, I shall consider again and again what she practiced in the ancient, holy place.

At her presentation, her spirit, her heart, her senses, all carried the imprint of the faithful love which she swore to the Lord in his sanctuary. It was a faithful love which served as a model for the women of Israel. Her piety and faithful love had no other motive than to please God, no other goal other than to hasten the coming of the Messiah. That was the desire of all nations.

Mary's faithful love rendered inaccessible the passions of the world. Faithful love divided out the holy work of her days between meditation on the laws, and her work in the Lord's house. After having been separated from her just and virtuous family, she did not cease to thank God for the pious teachings which she had received. Mary's faithful love prepared her soul for the sublime virtues, the singular graces which would shine forth from her soul for the rest of her years.

I considered what happiness there would be for me if I could imitate Mary by cultivating a faithful love, a love to seal my union with Jesus in the sacrament of the altar! What fruit would be produced in my soul by the frequent use of Communion! My love for God who gives himself to me carries me each time to new progress in piety! How this progress will be multiplied!

How the Lord will hear me in the regularity and fervor of my prayers, in the constancy and generosity of my resolutions, in the exact and severe vigilance I shall maintain in myself through the submission of my will. I shall remain disposed to the will of Providence through gracious charity for my fellow men and women, through constraining my desires. With Mary as my model, I will occupy myself more and more with God. More of me will then be conserved in his grace. With these traits, offered in imitation of Mary, I will manifest my faithful love.

PRAYERS OF VENERABLE MOTHER THÉRÈSE OF SAINT AUGUSTINE

Meditation on the Actions of the Graces of Eucharistic Jesus and a Prayer to the Holy Virgin

I HAVE A HEART, O MY JESUS! And is it not penetrated by the excellent gifts you have given me on this holy day? Delivered by your kind providence from the many dangers which possessed my childhood, I am allowed a life by a miracle of your protection. I was removed by a very merciful disposition on your part from risks and dangers in which my innocence could have been exposed and jeopardized.

I have experienced, from the dawn of my days, all that your love could testify of tenderness and predilection, my God! But these first pledges of your paternal attention do not suffice to show the extent of your charity. There was a sorrow in my first years that you later dispelled. The teachings of your holy religion were made tasty to my soul and you gave rise in me to an affectionate piety for the sacrament of your altar.

From the moment I received you and possessed you, a lively faith, an ardent faith increased my desires even more. You understand this, you granted my wishes, O God of bounty. You crowned them, in giving me your sacred body for nourishment. O favor! Until the last instant of my life, your gift will be cherished in my grateful heart! Engraved in my heart in strokes of love, it will prompt more fervent acts of grace , not only each year, but each day.

May I recall all of these graces, especially when I come to adore you in your sanctuary, or when I offer you my soul for your residence! I will say a thousand times, "Come, divine Jesus. Accept this heart that you have desired to closely unite with. Would that my heart would be all for you, that it would not look for any other love than yours, that it would have no life other than yours. With an attentive, generous, faithful love, may I respond always to your love in honor of your first visit.

O Mary, my tender mother, my kind patron, help me to fulfill these duties gratefully. Under your auspices and by your example, I presented myself to the Lord. I have begged him to pour into my heart your purity. Obtain for me the pardon of all my lukewarmness and inattention. These have created obstacles though each of my Communions serves as reparation. At each new Communion, guide me to a new fervor, a profound humility, a submissive faith, a persevering desire, a complete consecration of myself. Help me to receive the indulgences of my God, the increase of his graces, and an eternity of his reward. Amen.

~*MEDITATIONS EUCHARISTIQUES,* LOUISE OF FRANCE, PP. 41–48

8

Saint Margaret Redi of the Sacred Heart

FEAST DAY:
September 1

THERE WAS NO LACK OF DEVOTION to the Blessed Sacrament in the 1700s. On July 15, 1747, Anna Maria Redi was born. After a childhood spent in gazing on God in all things, and a loving desire for all things heavenly, she enjoyed constant union with God and yearned to receive him in the Blessed Sacrament from a younger age than was permitted. At the age of ten, she received the Eucharist for the first time.

After that, she was very careful to avoid any fault or sin, and inflicted many penances on herself to show her love for Christ. Teresa Margaret entered the Carmelite monastery in Florence at the age of seventeen. Because of Saint Teresa's great love of the Sacred Heart she was naturally drawn to devotion to the Blessed Sacrament, the Sacrament of Love or as she would say "our heaven on earth."

~*GOD IS LOVE*, P. 169

— ✤ —

WHEN THIS LITTLE SAINT ENTERED CARMEL, she was delighted to be able to receive the Eucharist twice a week, which was the custom at that time. It was said that she appeared radiant on days when she was able to receive the Blessed Sacrament. She was so attracted to the real presence that she would not only think of him frequently, but would turn her body toward the area of the tabernacle whenever possible.

Even at rest time, she would rest her head against the wall next to the chapel and face the tabernacle. When found in this manner she replied: "Truly God is here. I dwell in the very house of Jesus in the Blessed Sacrament. We must keep our eyes cast down and our hearts raised up to God!"

~*GOD IS LOVE*, P. 171

SAINT TERESA WAS BLESSED WITH THE GIFT of perceiving a special taste and fragrance when receiving Holy Communion. She thought everyone had this same experience. She referred to it as the "perfume of holiness." She asked her spiritual director, Father Idelphonse, why she sometimes felt it more and sometimes less. He questioned her: "In what does it consist, this taste you speak of?" She replied: "Why, I do not know how to explain. It is the savor of Jesus Christ, I suppose, as the psalm says: 'Taste and see that the Lord is sweet.'"

As to more or less degrees of tasting and smelling the host, Father told her, it could indicate greater or less fervor in the reception of Holy Communion.

~GOD IS LOVE, P. 172

TERESA MARGARET'S GREATEST JOY was to spend her time in silent adoration before the tabernacle. She loved to do this without being observed by anyone. Teresa once said: "I do not envy the angels in heaven apart from their enjoyment in the beatific vision. Do we not have God dwelling in our midst?"

~GOD IS LOVE, P. 173

TERESA KNEW LONG BEFORE HER FIRST COMMUNION that God was truly in the tabernacle. She used to exclaim: "May the Sacred Heart of Jesus in the Blessed Sacrament be praised, loved, and worshipped in all the tabernacles of the world. Ah, what continual irreverence he receives from man in his own house! In his humility, he deigns to dwell in our midst, yet how often is he neglected and forgotten, left in empty churches, while in his turn, he never grows weary of this lonely vigil. Truly 'Love is not loved!'"

~GOD IS LOVE, P. 175

SEVERAL OF THE SISTERS COMMENTED on how meticulously she performed every duty, never speaking to anyone in any of the rooms near the Blessed Sacrament. She particularly loved arranging flowers for the Lord's altar. Many times she had to care for her patients in the infirmary and did not have time to prepare for Holy Communion. Teresa's reply when help was offered would be: "Don't fret, I shall be deprived of nothing except perhaps a little leisure. As for preparation, can there be any better than the performance of duties given one by obedience, particularly when it is also serving the sick?"

Saint Teresa Margaret died March 7, 1770, with her crucifix pressed to her lips and her head turned slightly toward the Blessed Sacrament. Her body seemed to be quickly decomposing, and the funeral had to be held without delay. However, after Mass she began to turn back to her healthy hue and her limbs were once more supple and could be moved with ease. About Teresa was a wonderful fragrance even after the flowers wilted and turned to dust. It was the "odor of sanctity" that she spoke of in regard to her Eucharistic Jesus.

~*GOD IS LOVE*, P. **175**

9

Augustin-Marie of the Blessed Sacrament, O.C.D.

BORN IN 1821 TO A JEWISH FAMILY in Hamburg, Germany, Hermann Cohen converted to Catholicism in 1847, and soon after become a Carmelite friar. This came after spending years of living in a very worldly manner. He was best known as a composer who was a close friend of Franz Liszt.

Speaking about the change that took place in his spiritual life and led him into the Church, Hermann related:

"It happened in the month of May last year, 1847. Mary's month was celebrated with great pomp at the Church of Saint Valere. Various choirs were playing music and singing which drew people in. Prince Moskowa, who organized the music and who was known to me, asked me if I would stand in for him and direct the choirs. I agreed and went to take my place purely from my interest in music and a desire to do the job well. During the ceremony, nothing affected me much but at the moment of Benediction, though I was not kneeling like the congregation, I felt something deep within me as if I had found myself. It was like the prodigal son facing himself. I was automatically bowing my head."

Until the time of his Baptism, his conversion continued thus: "At the moment of Benediction I felt a very real emotion though I cannot describe it, as if I had no right to be taking part in the ceremony.

"When I returned the following Friday, the same thing happened and I thought of becoming a Catholic. A few days later, I was passing the same church of Saint Valere while the bell was ringing for Mass. I went in and attended Mass with devotion and stayed on for several more Masses, not understanding what was holding me there. Even when I came home that evening, I was drawn to return. Again, the church bell was ringing and the Blessed Sacrament was exposed. As soon as I saw it, I felt drawn to the altar rail and knelt down. I bowed my head at the moment of Benediction and afterwards I felt a new peace in my heart. I came home and went to bed and felt the same thing in my dreams. From then on, I was anxious to attend Mass often which I did at Saint Valere and always with an inner joy."

After his conversion, Augustin-Marie was so devoted to the Blessed Sacrament that he began the Nocturnal Adoration Society in 1848. His devotion to the Eucharist broke forth in music composed with this in mind. He helped in the foundation of several convents, and finally died of smallpox in 1871.

— ✢ —

On Eucharistic Theme

I know a secret key which never fails
To open the gates of divine mercy.
I know a river which will carry us
Into the promised land.
I know a palm-tree which will shelter us
From the burning heat of our earthly exile;
I know a spring whose refreshing waters slake
Our thirst in the desert of this life:
I know a star which will guide us
As the pillar of cloud guided Israel,
Across the sandy ocean of our existence
To the end of our journey.

I know a dew which God sheds from heaven
And which must sustain us for the remainder
Of the road we have to travel;

I know a tree whose wood can sweeten
The bitter waters which are our
Portion to drink here below,
And make them give us a foretaste
of the heavenly Canaan.
I know a victim whose sacrifice ascends
In an odor of sweetness to the
God of Abraham;

And this secret key,
This river,
This palm-tree,
This star,
This heavenly dew,
This holocaust,
Is the Eucharist

~STORY OF HERMANN COHEN, O.C.D.

Father Hermann often put his thoughts about the Eucharist into words and music:

MY WELL-BELOVED when all are asleep
And seem to forget your love
Do permit me to watch
Alone with you in this abode.
(Canticle he put to music in a collection called "Love of Jesus Christ")
~STORY OF HERMANN COHEN, O.C.D., P. 37

Hermann dedicated his hymns to the Eucharist in the following prayer:

OH JESUS MY LOVE, I should like to kindle in the hearts of my former friends the fire which burns in me. I should like to show them the happiness you give to me. . . . If you no longer see me trying my utmost for applause and empty respect, it is because I have found my renown in the Eucharist. . . . If you no longer see me wasting my resources in casinos or chasing riches, it is because I have found wealth and inexhaustible treasure in the cup of love sealed in the Eucharist.

If I no longer come and drown my worries in your noisy parties, it is because I have found true joy. Yes, I have found it, what I really love; it is mine and no one can take it from me. Unhappy riches, cloying pleasures, honors that only debase—those are the things I looked for in your company. But now that my eyes have seen, and my hands have touched and my heart has beaten on the heart of God, I can only be sorry for your blindness in pursuing pleasures that are unable to fill your hearts. So, come to this heavenly feast which has been prepared by eternal wisdom. Come, draw near. Abandon your baubles and empty dreams, cast off the rags that cover you. Ask Jesus for the shining robe of pardon. Then with a new heart, with a pure heart quench your thirst at the limpid fountain of his love. Cast yourselves down at his feet. Give your heart to him and he will bless you, and you will taste joys so great that I cannot describe them for you—unless you come and try them.

Taste and see how sweet is the Lord!

If King David danced before the ark which prefigured you, O my true covenant, then with what songs of triumphs ought I break out?

~*Story of Hermann Cohen*, O.C.D., P. 38

Another prayer from this Carmelite again shared his joy in the Eucharist:

HAVING LOOSENED WORLDLY BONDS, I can now penetrate the dark cloud that surrounds the tabernacle and open myself to the piercing rays from the sun of your grace, and plunge into the sea of light so as to be burnt in the flame of this blazing furnace. Then, taking shelter in the shade of this tree of life, I can taste its fruits. For me those days and nights pass joyfully in intimate converse with your adored presence, between the memory of today's Communion and the hope of tomorrow's, God united with the least of his children.

~*Story of Hermann Cohen*, O.C.D., P. 38

A Little Flower at the Door of the Tabernacle

(Motet composed without any instrumental resources while at Tarasteix)

Between two cold barriers there grew a little plant
Which brightened the tedium of the prisoner
Who cultivated it with love.
And in exchange for his care

He saw the humble plant
Emit with all its energy the fragrance
Of its flowers.

Ah, divine master
Within the tabernacle
A prisoner of love
For eighteen hundred years
In spite of our coldness, by a constant miracle
you have made your dwelling place with us.
And there are more neglected, more lonely still
Than the poor captive whose loneliness I lament.

Your tenderness implores from your faithless chil-
dren
The hearts which they refuse to give you.
As they abandon you, O God of my heart.
I will be for you, my Jesus,
Your humble little flower.
And tell me how to please you as a little flower.
Within your hands may I forget myself forever.

~STORY OF HERMANN COHEN, O.C.D., P. 89

JESUS SPEAKS:

Indeed it is in faith, in naked faith
That my hand has planted this little flower
Which will come to me in solitude unknown to all.

It will have no other sun except a gaze from my
heart.

In place of root in this frail flower
I wish to see hope in me which never fails
Infinite hope in my goodness,
The trust of a child who knows that he is loved.
And then its fruit will be a quality so pure
Which gazes only on God on earth as in heaven,
Which has eyes for no one else
Which turns to me for the fulfillment of its desires.

And so my plans being realized
It will have deserved the richest gifts I have.
On my sacred heart I will graft this lowly plant
And I will be happy to unite it to myself.

~STORY OF HERMANN COHEN, O.C.D., P. 90

Foreword to a Collection of Motets

ADORABLE SACRAMENT, BLESSED SPRING from which my dry
lips can drink the first fruits of eternal life, my heart is
filled with joy. I need to bless you and sing your prais-
es in songs of joy and thanksgiving. Indeed, I have
learnt that my brothers in Paris can now adore you
each day in the practice of perpetual adoration. The

church bells in the city are ringing, and processional banners go before you.

The Archbishop is promoting this devotion, calling Christians together to arrange the altars and asking the children to come and sing. He himself is taking part in this uninterrupted adoration from church to church, making it a kind of image of the eternal praise given by the blessed to God. . . . You have given me a God of love, the language of harmony. Am I to remain dumb and not use it? If your friends do their best to adore you, a divine sacrament, have I not also a "Hosanna" to sing to your glory and a palm branch to place beneath your feet? Adored Lord, I must unite my songs with the hymns of Paris! For it was in that great city, hidden in the Eucharist that you revealed the truth to me, and the first mystery you revealed was your real presence in the Blessed Sacrament. Even then, although I was still a Jew, I wished to present myself at the holy table and receive you.

I was anxious for baptism in order to be united to you. But I did indeed receive untold consolation from you. And when at last I could receive the heavenly banquet, I found there the strength I needed, and I was changed. It became my protection and treasure; I longed to drink that living water and I hungered for the bread of angels. I am now obliged to sing joyful hymns to you, because it was your sacrament which did all this, which turned me from what was a harmful to a frugal life, and from an extravagant life to one of a humbler kind. Not only have I made solemn vows which consecrate me to you in Mary's order and makes me your beloved forever, but you ask me out of your jealous love, to make a further vow appropriate to your divine sacrament, a vow which will bind me with indissoluble bonds to the love of love itself. (The vow referred to was Hermann's resolution never to preach without mentioning the Eucharist)

Carmelite Priory, Agen, March 1851

~STORY OF HERMANN COHEN, O.C.D., p. 110

In one of his sermons he prayed:

O JESUS PRESENT IN THE EUCHARIST, in the desert of this life, you appeared to me one day, you revealed to me your light, your greatness, and your beauty. You knew how to overcome all obstacles in one moment. Then, you drew me strongly to yourself and stirred in my spirit a hunger for the bread of life and a thirst in my heart for your precious blood. . . . then at last came the day when I received you which I remember so well.

~STORY OF HERMANN COHEN, O.C.D., P. 111

10

Blessed Mary of Jesus Crucified
(the "Little Arab")

FEAST DAY:
August 25

BORN IN 1846 IN ABELLIN overlooking Nazareth in Palestine, Mariam Bouardy was one of the more spiritually gifted Carmelites of her times. After the loss of her parents when she was just two, Mariam was raised by her uncle. She was put to work at thirteen and served as a cook for Madame Naggier.

Mariam longed for the Eucharist from the time she was seven years old. She begged the priest to give her Holy Communion, but he always waited. One day Mariam enveloped herself in a large veil to conceal her identity and managed to slip into the Communion line to receive. "The priest, who according to the Byzantine rite held in his hand the chalice in which were steeped the particles of consecrated bread, held out to Mariam the little spoon containing the sacred species.

"She received the sacrament of the Body and Blood of Christ. The young girl was radiant with happiness, and later acknowledged that she had seen Jesus give himself to her under the appearance of a most beautiful child." As was the custom of the day, she made her first solemn Communion at the age of twelve, but quietly received the Eucharist until that time.

During one of her first Communions there, she was rapt in ecstasy. Her mistress, when informed of it, came for her in a carriage. The phenomenon lasted four days, and the doctors couldn't make anything of it. She related later that she had been in heaven, hell, and purgatory. While in this ecstasy, she received the order to fast on bread and water for one year to expiate the sins of gluttony in the world and to wear poor clothing to expiate the sins of immodesty and luxury.

Although illiterate, Mariam composed poems and prayers that are lilting and sweet. In her Carmelite house, she was known as Sister Mary of Jesus Crucified. She possessed many charismatic gifts such as ecstasies, levitations, stigmata, bilocation, mysterious knowledge, and transpiercing of the heart. This little one only lived to be thirty-three. She died at the Carmel of Bethlehem, which she founded, in 1878.

~*Mariam, the Little Arab*, p. 6

Throughout her life, Mariam ceaselessly recommended frequent reception of Communion to the nuns. With her gift of poetry, the "Little Arab" sings of her love and need for Sweet Eucharistic Jesus.

To what shall I liken me?

To little birds in their nest

If the father and mother do not bring them food, they die of

hunger.

Thus is my soul without You, Lord; it does not have its

nourishment, it cannot live!

To what shall I liken me?

To the little grain of wheat cast into the earth. If the dew falls

not, if the sun does not warm it, the grain molds.

But if You give your dew and your sun, the little grain will be

refreshed and warmed; it will take root and will produce a

beautiful plant with many grains.

To what shall I liken me, Lord?

To a rose that is cut and left to dry up in the hand.
It loses its perfume; but if it remains on the rosebush,
it is always fresh and beautiful and keeps all its perfume.

Keep me, Lord, to give me life in You.

To what shall I liken You, Lord?

To the dove that feeds its little ones, to a tender
  mother who nourishes her little babe.

~MARIAM, THE LITTLE ARAB, P. 46

Tree of Life

Hail, hail, Tree of life,

  That gives us the fruit of life!

From the center of this earth

  My heart repines, my heart sighs out.

Oh! Who will give me wings

  To fly to my Beloved!

Hail, hail Tree of life,

  That gives us the fruit of life!

I see on thy leaves these words are written:

  Have no fear of anything!

Thy verdure says: Have *Hope*.

Thy branches tell me: *Charity*.

And Thy shade: *Humility*.

Hail, hail, Tree of life;

  In Thee I find the fruit of life.

From the center of this earth,

  My heart repines, my heart is longing.

Oh! Who will give me wings

To fly to my Beloved!
Hail, hail, blessed tree;
Thou bearest the fruit of life.
Under Thy shade, I wish to sigh;
   At thy feet, I wish to die.

~MARIAM, THE LITTLE ARAB, P. **48**

THE "LITTLE ARAB" spent two seasons in Hell. She was delivered from this torment on Sundays so that she could receive Holy Communion and have a brief time of calm.

~MARIAM, THE LITTLE ARAB, P. **52**

"DURING HER PRIVATE VISITS TO THE BLESSED SACRAMENT, she would be lost in God. It would also happen that, transported by a supernatural joy, she would dance before the altar in the middle of the choir. Then she would say: 'David danced before the Ark, and I dance before the tabernacle.'"

According to Father Lazare, the ecstatic would go and knock on the door of the tabernacle when she was singing of Love and say: "Wake up! Wake up! You are sleeping!"

~MARIAM, THE LITTLE ARAB, P. **116**

11

Sister Marie of the Sacred Heart
(Sister of Saint Thérèse of Lisieux)

ONE DOESN'T HEAR MUCH about the other blood sisters of Saint Thérèse. The Little Flower shines so brightly in the Martin family constellation that the others seem less dazzling. However, each member of the family was uniquely blessed by God. Marie was no exception. She was born in 1860, and was the oldest child of the Martin family. It was Marie who guessed the grace that Thérèse had received from the "ravishing smile of the Blessed Virgin." She was the one who gave all of her dolls and their clothes to Thérèse. As Thérèse's godmother, she prepared Thérèse for her First Holy Communion.

Marie's First Communion was advanced a year because her aunt, a nun, had become gravely ill. Since Marie was a favorite of the sick nun, it was planned to give her this consolation before death. The head-mistress of the boarding school Marie attended promised her that she would be permitted to make her First Communion early if she learned her lessons well. She went to the chaplain of the monastery to learn her catechism, and Marie really enjoyed this opportunity. When he asked questions the others could not answer, she would think, "Oh, how I wish he would ask me; I know it so well!" Many times, he did ask her. The venerable priest might well have called Marie "his little doctor."

In addition to this, Marie made many sacrifices to prepare herself for the fruitful reception of Jesus. "Deep down in my heart," she writes, "I told myself that our Lord had led the rest to believe that my aunt was going to die just because he was eager to give himself to me. This thought filled me with joy." And though family members were repeatedly told that the aunt could not recover without a miracle, Marie persevered in unshaken faith.

How devout was the First Communion of our little Marie! She seemed a little angel, and was so well prepared! Great also was her joy when she was selected to recite the Act of Faith which so well summed up the sentiments of her soul! But that evening, before going to sleep, she was heard weeping. The Mistress hastened to her side to learn the cause of her sorrow. Marie finally managed to sob: "It is because the day of my First Communion is over."

Marie was the first among all the Martin sisters to become a Carmelite. She entered the Carmel of Lisieux in 1886, and died in 1940.

— ✛ —

On July 5, 1898, Marie wrote to Pauline:

"I WAS PRAYING TO MY LITTLE THÉRÈSE [who had died in 1897] to prepare me to receive the good God, when I was seized with so lively and penetrating a faith that I wondered how I would manage to take a step toward the grill for Communion. Had I seen our Lord with my own eyes, I could not have had more faith. When I received the Sacred Host, I seemed to hear an interior voice telling me: 'This is your Creator, your God, your Father, and your Savior.' But that does not really express what I felt at the time. Ah! I felt as though I possessed *all things* in myself."

~*MARIE: SISTER OF SAINT THÉRÈSE*, P. **59**

12

Saint Thérèse of the Child Jesus and the Holy Face
Doctor of the Church

FEAST DAY:
October 1

THÉRÈSE MARTIN, THE "LITTLE FLOWER," was born in 1873 into a loving and holy family in Lisieux, France. She was the youngest of nine children, but four died in early infancy or childhood. Thérèse experienced the loss of her mother when she was only four years old, and this left a deep impression on her. It was to her dear sisters that she looked for comfort. As a child too young to receive Holy Communion, Thérèse would ask her sister Celine for some of the blessed bread from Church. With bread from home, she would pretend to prepare her own little Mass. She and her father, while living at Les Buissonnets, would take a walk and visit the Blessed Sacrament. It was during one such walk that she entered a Carmelite chapel for the first time. Thérèse yearned for her First Holy Communion; and she would not be disappointed.

"The time of my First Communion remains engraved indelibly in my heart as a memory without any clouds. It seems to me that I could not have been better disposed to receive him than I was, and all my spiritual trials had left me for nearly a whole year," she wrote.

~*STORY OF A SOUL,* P. **73**

— ❖ —

AH! HOW SWEET WAS THAT FIRST KISS OF JESUS! It was a kiss of love; I felt that I was loved, and I said: "I love you, and I give myself to you forever!" There were no demands made, no struggles, no sacrifices; for a long time now Jesus and poor little Thérèse looked at and understood each other. That day, it was no longer two, Thérèse had vanished as a drop of water is lost in the immensity of the ocean. Jesus alone remained; he was the Master, the King. Had not Thérèse asked him to take away her liberty, for her liberty frightened her? She felt so feeble and fragile that she wanted to be united forever to the divine strength! Her joy was too great, too deep for her to contain, and tears of consolation soon flowed, to the great consternation of her companions. They did not understand that all the joy of heaven having entered her heart, her exiled heart was unable to bear it without shedding tears.

Thérèse was not allowed to receive Communion frequently at first, and so it was to be a month before she made her second Communion. She had longed for this moment, and she was again filled with tears upon receiving Jesus. She felt ineffable sweetness and repeated to herself the words of Saint Paul: "It is no longer I that live, it is Jesus who lives in me!"

Her desire to receive Jesus grew more and more intense, and she received permission to go to Communion on all the principal feasts. At boarding school, Thérèse found her only solace in spending time before Jesus in the Blessed Sacrament.

~*Story of a Soul*, p. 77

Her poems and prayers reflect her deep love for this Holy Sacrament.

Living Bread

Living Bread, Bread of Heaven, Divine Eucharist,
O touching mystery produced by Love,
Come dwell within my heart, Jesus, my white Host . . .
Deign to unite me unto Thee, O holy and sacred
    Vine,

That my feeble branch may yield its fruit to Thee;
And I will offer Thee a gilded cluster . . .
This cluster of love of which the grapes are souls.

~*SPIRITUAL REALISM OF SAINT THÉRÈSE OF LISIEUX*, P. **44**

Feast of Corpus Christi, 1896
Heaven for Me! . . .

1 To bear the exile of this valley of tears
   I need the glance of my Divine Savior.
   This glance full of love has revealed its charms to
       me.
   It has made me sense the happiness of Heaven.
   My Jesus smiles at me when I sigh to him.
   Then I no longer feel my trial of faith.
   My God's Glance, his ravishing Smile,
       That is Heaven for me! . . .

2 Heaven for me is to be able to draw down on souls,
   On the Church, my mother, and on all my sisters
   Jesus' graces and his Divine flames
   That can enkindle and rejoice hearts.
   I can obtain everything when mysteriously
   I speak heart to heart with my Divine King.
   That sweet prayer so near the Sanctuary,
       That is Heaven for me! . . .

3 Heaven for me is hidden in a little Host
Where Jesus, my Spouse, is veiled for love.
I go to that divine Furnace to draw out life,
And there my Sweet Savior listens to me night and
day.
"Oh! What a happy moment when in your
tenderness
You come, my Beloved, to transform me into
yourself.
That union of love, that ineffable intoxication,
That is Heaven for me!" . . .

4 Heaven for me is feeling within myself the
resemblance
Of the God who created me with his Powerful
Breath.
Heaven for me is remaining always in his presence,
Calling him my Father and being his child.
In his Divine arms, I don't fear the storm.
Total abandonment is my only law.
Sleeping on his Heart, right next to his Face,
That is Heaven for me! . . .

5 I've found my Heaven in the Blessed Trinity
That dwells in my heart, my prisoner of love.
There, contemplating my God, I fearlessly tell him
That I want to serve him and love him forever.
Heaven for me is smiling at this God whom I adore
When he wants to hide to try my faith.
To suffer while waiting for him to look at me again
   That is Heaven for me!

~*POETRY OF SAINT THÉRÈSE OF LISEUX*, PP. **153–155**

My Desires Near Jesus Hidden in His Prison of Love

1 Little Key, oh, I envy you!
For each day you can open
The prison of the Eucharist
Where the God of Love resides.
But, O what a sweet miracle!
By just an effort of my faith
I can also open the tabernacle
To hide near the Divine King.

2 Being consumed near my God
In the sanctuary, I would like
To burn forever with mystery
Like the Lamp of the Holy Place . . .

Oh! What happiness . . . I have flames within me,
And each day I can win
A great number of souls for Jesus,
Inflaming them with His love . . .

3 At each daybreak I envy you,
O Sacred Altar Stone!
As in the blessed stable,
On you the Eternal One wants to be born . . .
Ah! Deign to grant my prayer.
Come into my soul, Sweet Savior . . . Far from
being a cold stone,
It is the sigh of your Heart!

4 O Corporal surrounded by angels!
How enviable is your lot.
On you, as in his humble swaddling clothes,
I see Jesus, my only treasure.
Virgin Mary, change my heart
Into a pure, beautiful Corporal
To receive the white host,
Where your Sweet Lamb hides.

5 Holy Paten, I envy you.
Upon you Jesus comes to rest
Oh! May his infinite grandeur
Deign to humble itself even to me . . .
Fulfilling my hope, Jesus

Does not wait until the evening of my life.
He comes within me; by his presence
I am a living Monstrance! . . .

6 Oh! How I envy the happy chalice
Where I adore the divine Blood . . .
But at the Holy Sacrifice
I can take it in each morning.
To Jesus my soul is dearer
Than precious vessels of gold.
The Altar is a new Calvary
Where his Blood still flows for me . . .

7 Jesus, holy and sacred Vine,
O my Divine King, You know
I am a cluster of golden grapes
Which must disappear for you.
Under the wine press of suffering,
I shall prove my love for you.
I want no other joy
Than to sacrifice myself each day.
Ah! What joy I am chosen
Among the grains of pure Wheat
Who lose their lives for Jesus . . .
My delight is truly great! . . .
I am your dear spouse,
My Beloved, come live in me,

Oh! Come, your beauty has ravished me,
Deign to transform me into You!

~*POETRY OF SAINT THÉRÈSE OF LISIEUX,* PP. 133–135

The Sacristans of Carmel

Here below our sweet office
Is to prepare for the altar
The bread and wine of the Sacrifice
    Which brings "Heaven" to earth!

O supreme mystery, Heaven
Hides in humble bread,
For Heaven is Jesus Himself,
    Coming to us each morning.

There are no queens on earth
Who are happier than we.
Our office is a prayer
    Which unites us to our Spouse.

This world's greatest honors
Cannot compare
To the deep, celestial peace
    Which Jesus lets us savor.

We bring a holy envy
For the work of our hands,

For the little white host
   Which is to veil our divine Lamb.

But his love has chosen us,
He is our Spouse, our Friend.
We are also hosts
   Which Jesus wants to change into Himself.

Sublime mission of the Priest,
You become our mission here below.
Transformed by the Divine Master,
   It is He who guides our steps.

We must help the apostles
By our prayers, our love.
Their battlefields are ours.
   For them we fight each day.

The hidden God of the tabernacle
Who also hides in our hearts,
O what a miracle! At our voice
   Deigns to pardon sinners!

Our happiness and our glory
Is to work for Jesus.
His beautiful Heaven is the ciborium
We want to fill with souls!

~POETRY OF SAINT THÉRÈSE OF LISIEUX, PP. 170–171

Prayer to Jesus in the Tabernacle

O GOD HIDDEN IN THE PRISON OF THE TABERNACLE! I come with joy to you each evening to thank you for the graces you have given me. I ask pardon for the faults I committed today, which has just slipped away like a dream. . . .

O Jesus! How happy I would be if I had been faithful, but alas! Often in the evening I am sad because I feel I could have corresponded better with your graces. . . . If I were more united to you, more charitable with my sisters, more humble and more mortified, I would feel less sorrow when I talk with you in prayer. And yet, O my God, very far from becoming discouraged at the sight of my miseries, I come to you with confidence, recalling that "Those who are well do not need a doctor but the sick do."

I beg you, then, to cure me and to pardon me. I will keep in mind, Lord, "That the soul to whom you have forgiven more should also love you more than the others!" . . . I offer you every beat of my heart as so many acts of love and reparation and I unite them to your infinite merits. I beg you, O my Divine Bridegroom, to be the restorer of my soul, to act in me despite my resistance; and lastly I wish to have no other will but yours. Tomorrow, with the help of your grace, I will begin a new life in which each moment will be an act of love and renunciation.

Thus, after coming each evening to the foot of your altar, I will finally reach the last evening of my life. Then will begin for me the unending day of eternity when I will place in your divine heart the struggles of exile! Amen.

~*PRAYERS OF SAINT THÉRÈSE OF LISIEUX*, PP. 75–76

Behold, thy prisoner am I;
　　I, too, cry ever unto thee
Thine own divine and tender cry:
　　"I thirst! O let me die
Of love for thee!"

~*THE LITTLE FLOWER AND THE BLESSED SACRAMENT*, P. 30

It was not her own delight, however that she sought in this love, but the delight of her divine spouse. The cross and the Eucharist she holds as her dearest treasures upon earth. She compares them to the riches of her Guardian Angel:

Thine are Heaven's glory and delight:
　　The riches of the King of kings;
The host in our ciboriums bright
　　Is mine, and all the wealth pain brings.
So with the cross, and with the host,
　　And with thine aid, dear Angel Friend,
I wait in peace on time's dark coast
　　Heaven's happiness that knows no end.

~*THE LITTLE FLOWER AND THE BLESSED SACRAMENT*, P. 31

Thérèse wanted only to do God's will and would not ask to have her time on earth shortened.

Beyond the gloomy cloud
    Ever the skies are fair,
And angels sing aloud,
    And God is reigning there;
And yet without a tear
    I wait that bliss above,
Who in the host have here
    The perfect fruit of love.

~ *The Little Flower and the Blessed Sacrament*, p. 32

At the age of fifteen Thérèse wrote this letter about frequent reception of the Eucharist to Marie Guerin. It bears an Imprimatur of the Holy See!

BEFORE YOU CONFIDED IN ME, I felt that you were suffering, and my heart was one with yours. Since you have the humility to ask advice of your little Teresa, this is what she thinks: You have grieved me greatly by abstaining from Holy Communion, because you have grieved our Lord. The devil must be very cunning to deceive a soul in this way. Do you not know, dear Marie, that by acting thus you help him to accomplish his end?

The treacherous creature knows quite well that when a soul is striving to belong wholly to God he cannot cause her to sin, so he merely tries to persuade her that she has sinned. This is a considerable gain, but not enough to satisfy his hatred, so he aims at something more, and tries to shut out Jesus from a tabernacle which Jesus covets. Unable to enter this sanctuary himself, he wishes that at least it remain empty and without its God. Alas, what will become of that poor little heart? When the devil has succeeded in keeping a soul from Holy Communion he has gained all his ends . . . while Jesus weeps! . . .

Remember little Marie, that this sweet Jesus is there in the tabernacle expressly for you and you alone. Remember that he burns with the desire to enter your heart. Do not listen to Satan. Laugh him to scorn, and go without fear to receive Jesus, the God of peace and of love.

"Teresa thinks all of this," you say, "because she does not know my difficulties." She does know, and knows them well; she understands everything, and she tells you confidently that you can go without fear to receive your only true friend. She, too, has passed through the martyrdom of scruples, but Jesus gave her the grace to receive the Blessed Sacrament always, even when she imagined she had committed great sins. I assure you I have found that this is the only means of ridding oneself of the devil. When he sees that he is losing his time he leaves us in peace.

In truth it is impossible that a heart which can only find its rest in contemplation of the Tabernacle—and yours is such, you tell me—could so far offend our Lord as not to be able to receive him. . . . What does offend Jesus, what wounds him to the heart, is want of confidence.

Pray much that the best portion of your life may not be overshadowed by idle fears. We have only life's brief moments to spend for the glory of God, and well does Satan know it. This is why he employs every ruse to make us consume them in useless labor. Dear sister, go often to Holy Communion, go very often—that is your one remedy.

~*THE LITTLE FLOWER AND THE BLESSED SACRAMENT*, P.101

She writes in another place:

I CANNOT RECEIVE THEE IN HOLY COMMUNION as often as I should wish, but, O Lord, art thou not all-powerful? Abide in me as thou dost in the tabernacle—never abandon thy little victim.

~*THE LITTLE FLOWER AND THE BLESSED SACRAMENT*, P. 104

Thérèse had the privilege of receiving daily Communion when there was an epidemic. This sustained her and consoled her.

DURING ALL THESE LONG AND TRYING WEEKS I had the unspeakable consolation of receiving Holy Communion every day. How sweet it was! For a long time, Jesus treated me as a spoiled child, for a longer time than his more faithful spouses. He came to me daily for several months after the influenza had ceased, a privilege not granted to the community. I had not asked for this favor, but I was unspeakably happy to be united day after day to my Beloved.

~*The Little Flower and the Blessed Sacrament*, P. 105

Thérèse's love for Sweet Jesus in the Blessed Sacrament is expressed in her final days on earth in these words:

June 12, 1897

THEY DON'T BELIEVE I'M AS SICK AS I AM. So it makes it all the harder to be deprived of Holy Communion, the divine office. However, it's all the better if no one worried about me.

~*Saint Thérèse of Lisieux: Her Last Conversations*, P. 64

July 2, 1897

SHE WENT FOR THE LAST TIME BEFORE THE BLESSED SACRAMENT in the oratory in the afternoon; but she was at the end of her strength. I saw her look at the host for a long time and I guessed it was without any consolation but with much peace in her heart.

I recall that in the morning after the Mass, when the community was going to the oratory to make thanksgiving, no one thought of helping her. She walked very quietly close to the wall. I didn't dare offer her my arm.

~*Saint Thérèse of Lisieux: Her Last Conversations*, P. 64

July 30, 1897

She was showing us her hands with reverence after the Extreme Unction. I was collecting as usual the little pieces of skin from her desiccated lips, but that day she said to me: "I was swallowing my little skins today because I've received Extreme Unction and Holy Viaticum."

It was afternoon. She had hardly any time to make her thanksgiving when some sisters came to see her. She told me in the evening:

"How they came to disturb me after Communion! They stared me in the face . . . but in order not to be provoked, I thought of our Lord who retreated into solitude and was unable to prevent the people from following him there. And he didn't want to send them away. I wanted to imitate him by receiving the sisters kindly.

~Saint Thérèse of Lisieux: Her Last Conversations, p. 121

July, 1897

At Carmel, her great suffering had been not being able to receive Communion each day. She said, a short time before her death, to Mother Marie de Gonzague, who was afraid of daily Communion: "Mother, when I'm in heaven, I'll make you change your opinion."

This is what happened. After the death of the Servant of God, the chaplain gave us Communion every day, and Mother Marie de Gonzague, instead of being repelled by it, was very happy about it. (Thérèse entered the joy of her Lord on September 30, 1897.)

~*SAINT THÉRÈSE OF LISIEUX: HER LAST CONVERSATIONS*, P. 262

13

Blessed Elizabeth of the Trinity

ELIZABETH CATEZ was born in Dijon, France, in 1880. Her father was in the military, and she and her younger sister "Guite" were blessed with a happy home. At an early age, Elizabeth learned to pray and even tried to teach her dolls to do so! She enjoyed sewing, as can be seen in a picture of her and her sister in which they are wearing matching blouses that Elizabeth had made. A lively, popular girl and a gifted pianist, Elizabeth attended parties but her heart was always focused within—where the Trinity dwelled.

From an early age, Blessed Elizabeth was drawn to the Blessed Sacrament. On April 19, 1891, at age eleven, she made her First Holy Communion. That was a real turning point in her life. She died at twenty-six years of age of Addison's disease, but in her short life, God raised her to the heights of holiness in Carmel. She always remembered her First Communion day and its impact.

". . . That day when Jesus made His dwelling within me, when God took possession of my heart so completely and so well that since that hour, since that mysterious colloquy, that divine delightful converse, I have aspired only to give my life, to return a little of His great love to the Beloved of the Eucharist who rests in my poor heart, inundating it with all his favors." April 19, 1898 (p. 47 Letters).

~*LIGHT, LOVE, LIFE: ELIZABETH OF THE TRINITY,* P. **36**

— ❖ —

Seven years after her First Holy Communion Elizabeth commemorated her first encounter with Christ in a poem of gratitude and praise:

Sweet birds, nature's cantors,
Mountains and hills, flowers and greenery,
Stars shining brightly in the blue sky,
You sun, glowing like a disc of fire,
You beautiful sea with foam covered waves,
You fertile and resplendent land,
All of you, God's masterpieces,
Sing with me in unison!
. . . On this anniversary of the day
on which Jesus made his home within me,

on which God took possession of my heart,
So much so that since that hour . . .
I have no wish but to give my life to him,
To render thanks to him for his great love . . .
To him who floods me with favors.
Do you recall, Jesus, who are so full of charm,
My pure and joyous tears
Which flowed with such sweetness
Over your divine feet and over your heart?
That blessed day, the most beautiful day of my life.

~ *QUEEN ELIZABETH OF THE TRINITY: EUCHARISTIC VICTIM*

For forty hours devotions in Lent of 1899, she wrote:

Perpetual Adoration

O Jesus of the Eucharist,
My spouse, my love, my life,
How I love to listen to you,
To speak to you, to see you every evening.
O, how sweet are these encounters,
How sweet are these tears . . .
You, my supreme love, O my king,
My Jesus, captive and solitary,
When I am near you,
It seems to me that I am no longer on earth.
When I hear your voice,

O my spouse, O my good master,
My whole being is silenced.
I hear and see nothing but you.
O those sublime, ecstatic moments,
Intimate and sweet union,
When my heart beats in unison with my savior!
Would that I could spend
Long hours in that holy abode.
Would that I could live eternally close to Jesus,
My sole love . . .
Nothing keeps me on earth.
Jesus alone can satisfy me.
Apart from Jesus, I care for nothing.
He is my treasure, my sole wealth.
Near to him I am happy.
He is my life and my love.
For him I am eager to suffer, yes, to suffer for ever!
O, to suffer and to console his heart,
Crushed by pain!
To suffer and to prove thereby that I love him,
Jesus, my only love!
Jesus, God of the Eucharist!
Jesus, my sustenance, my life!
Jesus who deigns to choose me,
That I may love him, console him
And suffer with and for him.

~*Queen Elizabeth of the Trinity: Eucharistic Victim*

OH! WHAT THREE DELIGHTFUL DAYS I HAVE JUST SPENT! In the evening, I made a good half hour of adoration before the Blessed Sacrament until the divine office at 8:00. Who could describe the sweetness of this heart-to-heart encounter in which one feels no longer on earth, and no longer sees nor hears anything but God! God who speaks to the soul; God who communicates to it such sweet things; God who asks it to suffer! In short, Jesus, who desires a little love. . . . February 12, 1899 (D8).

~LIGHT, LOVE, LIFE: ELIZABETH OF THE TRINITY, P. 52

EVERY SUNDAY, WE HAVE THE BLESSED SACRAMENT exposed in the oratory. When I open the door and contemplate the divine prisoner who has made me a prisoner in this dear Carmel, it seems to me rather like the gate of Heaven opening! Then I present to Jesus all those who are in my heart, and there, close to him, I find them again.

Sept. 11, 1901 (L 91).

~LIGHT, LOVE, LIFE: ELIZABETH OF THE TRINITY, P. 71

January 1, 1904

To her mother:

. . . I SPENT A HEAVENLY DAY CLOSE to the Blessed Sacrament, and I took you with me, for you know very well I never leave you. I am so happy about the nice day you had (L189).

~LIGHT, LOVE, LIFE: ELIZABETH OF THE TRINITY, P. 141

June 14, 1903

To Abbe Chevignard:

IT SEEMS TO ME THAT NOTHING BETTER EXPRESSES THE LOVE in God's heart than the Eucharist. It is union, consummation; he is in us, we in him. And isn't that heaven on earth, heaven in faith while awaiting the face-to-face vision we so desire.

During that whole octave, we have the Blessed Sacrament exposed in the oratory. Those are divine hours spent in this little corner of heaven where we possess the vision in substance under the humble host. Yes, he whom the blessed contemplate in light, and we adore in faith is really the same one.

~LIGHT, LOVE, LIFE: ELIZABETH OF THE TRINITY, P. 105

"HE WHO EATS MY FLESH AND DRINKS MY BLOOD, remains in Me and I in him." "The first sign of love is this: that Jesus has given us his flesh to eat and his blood to drink." The property of love is to be always giving and receiving. Now the love of Christ is generous. All that he has, all that he is, he gives; all that we have, all that we are, he takes away. He asks for more than we of ourselves are capable of giving. He has an immense hunger which wants to devour us absolutely. He enters even into the marrow of our bones, and the more lovingly we allow him to do so, the more fully we savor him. He knows that we are poor, but he pays no heed to it and does not spare us.

He himself becomes in us his own bread, first burning up, in his love, all our vices, faults and sins. Then, when he sees that we are pure, he comes like a gaping vulture that is going to devour everything. He wants to consume our life in order to change it into his own; ours, full of vices, his, full of grace and glory and all prepared for us, if only we will renounce ourselves. Even if our eyes were good enough to see this avid appetite of Christ who hungers for our salvation, all our efforts would not prevent us from disappearing into his open mouth. Now, this sounds absurd, but those who love will understand! When we receive Christ with interior devotion, his blood, full of warmth and glory, flows into our veins and a fire is enkindled in our depths. We receive the likeness of his virtues, and he lives in us and we in him. He gives us his soul with the fullness of grace, by which the soul perseveres in love and praise of the Father!

Love draws its object into itself; we draw Jesus into ourselves; Jesus draws us into himself. Then carried above ourselves into love's interior, seeking God, we go to meet him, to meet his Spirit, which is his love, and this love burns us, consumes us, and draws us into unity where beatitude awaits us. Jesus meant this when he said: "With great desire have I desired to eat this Pasch with you."

~COLLECTED WORKS OF ELIZABETH OF THE TRINITY,

VOLUME 1, P. 100

14

Blessed Titus Brandsma

FEAST DAY:
July 27

TITUS BRANDSMA was born in the Netherlands in 1881. He joined the Carmelites when he was still young. After being ordained in 1905, he studied in Rome and earned his doctorate in theology. He was also a journalist, philosopher, and a linguist. Because he wrote in opposition to anti-Jewish marriage laws, he came to the attention of the Nazis. He was arrested in 1942 when he wrote that no Catholic publication could justify the publication of Nazi propaganda.

When interred in Nazi concentration camps, he longed for this food of the strong, of which he was often deprived. He was overjoyed when on occasion he was able to obtain a tiny particle of the Eucharist, keep it with him during the night, adoring Christ present even in that epitome of inhumanity, until the next morning when he could receive Communion. His favorite prayer became the *Adoro te devote*.

In Dachau, one day Father Titus was fortunate enough to secure a small particle of the Eucharist. He placed it in his eyeglass case and hid it under his arm. The head of the barracks was not satisfied with Father Titus' appearance and began beating him, using foul language, knocking him down, striking him repeatedly until the priest was bloody. When he had vented his spleen, a fellow prisoner helped the dazed Father Titus to his feet and to his cot and mentioned, "You must be in terrible pain."

Father Titus responded, "Not really, Brother," he pointed to the eyeglass case and smilingly added: "I knew whom I had with me. Join me in an *Adoro te devote*, won't you?" And as he could not sleep during the night, Fr. Titus kept vigil all night in adoration. He was killed at Dachau concentration camp in July of 1942 with a lethal injection.

~*Beatification of Blessed Titus Brandsma*, P. 117

— ✤ —

Some of his recorded teachings on the Blessed Sacrament came from a retreat:

IN SPEAKING OF THE CARMELITES' TENDER DEVOTION to the Sacrament of the Altar, it goes without saying that we do not wish to imply that it is peculiar to them, but only to point out some of the remarkable aspects of it. They have always seen a symbol of the sacred host in the wonderful food which the angel pointed out to Elijah and which strengthened the prophet in finding the way that he was able to cross the desert and reach Mount Horeb. The Eucharist is the power which permits them to arrive at contemplation. The rule already prescribed daily assistance at Mass and the construction of an oratory in the middle of the cells. The history of the order furnishes admirable models of devotion.

Saint Peter Thomas who died in 1365 was prior general at the time of the Avignon popes. He was also Patriarch of Constantinople and Apostolic delegate of Pope Clement for the East at the time of the crusade against Alexandria. He was not hindered by the many occupations of his busy life from spending several hours each night before the Blessed Sacrament; oftentimes he was found lost in adoration.

Blessed John Soreth . . . a great reformer of the Carmelites in the fifteenth century, his life imperiled, grasped the Blessed Sacrament from the hands of sacrilegious men and rescued it from a burning church. At the end of that century, Blessed Bartholomew Fanti, who counted Blessed Baptist Spagnoli among his disciples, taught his novices that it was not possible to be a good Carmelite without special devotion to the Blessed Sacrament. He cured the sick with a touch of the sanctuary lamp. What determined Saint Mary Magdalen de' Pazzi to enter the Carmel of Florence was the

practice of daily Communion observed in this convent—
a thing rare for the times.

The Carmelites are rightly numbered among the
mendicant orders, for their constitutions demand the
greatest simplicity in their monasteries. But for their
churches and the cult of the Eucharist, grandeur was
always permitted. The documents establishing several
houses give as the reason for foundation the desire of
assuring splendor for the liturgical ceremonies. In
Carmelite churches, the scene of Elijah in the desert
represented in painting or sculpture is permitted.

Day X: Final Meditation
Renewal of Vows

WE SHOULD SEE THE MASS as the expression of our sacrifice to God and Holy Communion as its complement.
"Do this in memory of Me" (Lk 22:19; 1 Cor 11:24). At
the Last Supper, he gave himself to us as food. On the
cross, he finalized his sacrifice, which is renewed in the
Mass.

At the offertory, when the matter of sacrifice is on
the paten and in the chalice, let us offer ourselves to
God as well, so that he who transforms and changes the
bread and wine into the flesh and blood of Jesus, also
change us to the degree that we may say with Saint
Paul, "I live, no not I, but Christ lives in me" (Gal 2:20).

During Mass, we call down the blessing of God on our offerings. "Let my prayer rise as incense in your sight" (Ps 140:2). The priest incenses the offerings, for matter of sacrifice, saying these sublime words: "May this incense, blessed by you, O Lord, rise before you, and may your mercy come down on us." . . .

Holy Communion is the seal on our vows.

~*ESSAYS ON TITUS BRANDSMA*

15

Blessed Mother Maria Candida of the Eucharist

FEAST DAY:
June 14

MARIA BARBA was born in Catazara, Italy, in 1884, to a deeply religious family. Maria desired to receive Holy Communion long before the age allowed at that time. She would run to greet her mother after she would return from Mass and kiss her. Then she would joyfully exclaim: "I have received God too!" After her First Communion, to be deprived of it was a great and painful cross.

After twenty years of waiting and longing, she entered the Carmel in Ragusa, Italy, taking the name Maria Candida of the Eucharist. The reason for the delay was the vehement opposition of her parents.

Maria Candida had a very intense devotion to the Eucharist, and believed that this devotion would be her special vocation. Mother was prioress for many years, and made a new foundation in Syracuse. She died in 1949, and was beatified in 2004.

— ✠ —

IN THE EUCHARIST (Colloqui Eucaristici) she gives a lengthy, deep meditation on the Eucharist:

I would like to be like Mary, to be Mary for Jesus, to take the place of his Mamma. I have Mary also present in my communions. I want to receive Jesus from her hands. She must help me to become only one thing with him. I know that I cannot separate Mary from Jesus. Hail, O Body born of Mary! Hail Mary, dawn of the Eucharist!

~ COLLOQUI EUCARISTICI

THE LOVELINESS OF THE EUCHARIST, the sweetness of its symbol, my Jesus in person there on his throne: and then the greatness, the splendors of the Church, of all religion, the magnificence of the cult, the holiness of the sacred ministers, the incalculable treasure of the word of Jesus, all was before me, while my soul was languishing like it was captivated in admiration, holy astonishment, immense gratitude and sweet delight. O Jesus, Jesus, how well you made everything. What splendor is your religion! What is this Church that you came to found? O marvels, O the magnitude of your work, truly divine things!

~Colloqui Eucaristici

The Eucharist and Faith

O my Beloved Jesus in the Blessed Sacrament, I see you, I believe in you! Although you are hidden from me under the Eucharistic veils, by the sweet ciborium, by the little door of the tabernacle, by the grate, the wall, I see you. I believe in you all the more!

O holy faith!

~Colloqui Eucaristici, pp. 117, 118

The Eucharist and Hope

O my divine Eucharist, my dear hope! I await all from you—from you the work of my sanctification, for your divine thunderbolts that must destroy and finish me. From you heaven, to you my past, my present and my future!

O sweet hope!

~Colloqui Eucaristici, pp. 125, 126

The Eucharist and Charity

MY JESUS, HOW MUCH I LOVE YOU: It is an immense love that is bound up in my heart for you, O sacramental love. My heart is destroyed with tenderness for you. Measure out how much of this, my love, you want. O Lord, this my love; measure out! When you have so much, so much of it, measure [it] out. When it seems to have finished, I must begin again. And this so often, always, because with infinite love (forgive me) I love you!

~*COLLOQUI EUCARISTICI*, PP. 133, 134

The Eucharist and Reparation

O MY BELOVED IN THIS HOLY SACRAMENT, how much I am tormented, how much agony I must bring to mind, to see the sight of the offenses that you bear in this most august sacrament. I would like to make a shield of myself. I would receive it all myself. O heavenly Father, think about your only-begotten son made bread, for men. O holy angel of the tabernacle, guard such a treasure and do not allow those who profane, the stained souls to come near!

Accept this reparation, my love!

~*COLLOQUI EUCARISTICI*, P. 157

16

Saint Teresa Benedicta of the Cross

FEAST DAY:
August 9

BORN IN 1891 INTO A JEWISH FAMILY in Breslau, Germany, Edith Stein was raised in a deeply religious environment. However, she abandoned the faith of her youth, and lived exploring and searching for the truth. This led her to study of phenomenology under the renowned Dr. Edmund Husserl. But she had a conversion experience one night after reading Saint Teresa of Avila's autobiography. She exclaimed, "That is the truth!" Shortly after that, she was baptized a Catholic and received her First Communion.

Later, she had a great desire to become a Carmelite nun, but because of her mother's terrible grief over her conversion, she waited. A few years later, she entered the Carmel of Cologne, taking the name Sister Teresa Benedicta of the Cross. The Nazi persecution prompted her to ask for a transfer to the Carmel of Echt in Holland. She wanted to protect her Carmelite sisters in Germany. Nonetheless, Sister Teresa Benedicta and her own blood sister, Rosa Stein, were arrested by the Nazis because of their Jewish origins and taken to Auschwitz in August 1942. The two of them were executed a week after their arrest.

Since her canonization in 1998, Saint Teresa Benedicta of the Cross is being discovered by more and more people. Her writings provide a great legacy and give testimony to her Eucharistic devotion.

Saint Teresa Benedicta gave advice to some working women about how they could accomplish all that they needed to do within the day:

"So I will go to the altar of God"(Ps. 43:4). Here it is not a question of my minute, petty affairs, but of the great offering of reconciliation. I may participate in that, purify myself and be made happy, and lay myself with all my doings and troubles along with the sacrifice on the altar. And when the Lord comes to me then in Holy Communion, then I may ask him, "Lord, what do you want of me?" (St Teresa). And after quiet dialogue, I will go to that which I see as my next duty.

I will still be joyful when I enter into my day's work after this morning's celebration: my soul will be empty of that which could assail and burden it, but it will be filled with holy joy, courage and energy.

Because my soul has left itself and entered into the divine life, it has become great and expansive. Love burns in it like a composed flame which the Lord has enkindled, and which urges my soul to render love to inflame love in others. And it sees clearly the next part of the path before it; it does not see very far, but it knows that when it has arrived at that place where the horizon now intersects, a new vista will then be opened.

~*EDITH STEIN: ESSENTIAL WRITINGS*, P. 65

— ✤ —

COMMUNION DELIVERS US FROM EVIL, because it cleanses us of sin and gives us peace of heart that takes away the sting of all other "evils." It brings us the forgiveness of past sins and strengthens us in the face of temptations. It is itself the bread of life that we need daily to grow into eternal life. It makes our will into an instrument at God's disposal. Thereby, it lays the foundation for the kingdom of God in us and gives us clean lips and a pure heart to glorify God's holy name. Participation in the sacrifice and in the sacrificial meal actually transforms the soul into a living stone in the city of God—in fact, each individual soul—into a temple of God.

~*EDITH STEIN: ESSENTIAL WRITINGS*, PP. 48–49

IN CARMEL, SAINT TERESA BENEDICTA continued her studies and writing. She wrote "On the History and Spirit of Carmel." In this essay she places adoration of the Blessed Sacrament at the heart of the Carmelite vocation. She is realistic concerning the practical needs of life, yet to stand before the face of God is the real content of the Carmelite's life.

But we have the Savior not only in the form of reports of witnesses to his life. He is present in the Most Blessed Sacrament. The hours of adoration before the Highest Good, and listening for the voice of the Eucharistic God, are simultaneously meditation on the law of the Lord and watching in prayer. But the highest level is reached when the law is deep within our hearts (Ps 40:8), when we are so united with the triune God, whose temple we are, that his Spirit rules all we do or omit.

~BLESSED EDITH STEIN AND THE EUCHARIST

The Bread of Life

THE SAVIOUR, KNOWING THAT WE ARE and continue to be men who have daily to struggle with our weakness, aids our humanity in a manner truly divine. Just as our earthly body requires daily bread, so the divine life in us must be fed continually. This is the living bread which has come down from heaven. If we make it truly our daily food, the mystery of Christmas, the

Incarnation of the Word, will be enacted again each day in us. And this, it seems to me, is the best way to remain in constant union with God, and to grow each day more securely and deeply into the Mystical Body of Christ.

~EDITH STEIN IN HER WRITINGS, P. 4

Nourished on the Eucharist

ONLY BY THE POWER OF GRACE can nature be purged from its dross and made ready to receive the divine life. And this life itself is the fountain from which springs the works of love. A woman's life for which divine love is to be the driving force will have to be a Eucharistic life. To forget self, to open one's heart to the various needs of others—this becomes possible only through daily intimacy with our Lord in the tabernacle.

If we visit the Eucharistic God and seek his counsel in all our problems, if we let ourselves be purified by the sanctifying power that flows from the altar, if we offer ourselves to the Lord in this sacrifice and receive him into our souls in Holy Communion, then we cannot but be drawn ever more deeply into the current of the divine life. We shall grow into the mystical body of Christ and our heart will be fashioned in the likeness of the Sacred Heart.

~EDITH STEIN IN HER WRITINGS, P. 21

Letter to Elly Dursy
(Sister Maria Elisabeth of Divine Providence, O.C.D)

Pax!

Dear Elly,

As I have just come up from the Chapel where the Most Blessed Sacrament is exposed (and where *coram Sanctissimo* [before the Most Holy] a choral High Mass was sung—a horrendous thing for an ultra-liturgist!), I would like to bring you greetings from our Eucharistic Savior, and at the same time, an affectionate reproach for letting yourself be led astray by a few printed words about something you have experienced before the tabernacle for so many years.

Dogmatically, I believe the matter is very clear: the Lord is present in the tabernacle in his divinity and in his humanity. He is not present for his own sake but ours: it is his delight to be with the "children of men." He knows too that, being what we are, we need his personal nearness. In consequence, every thoughtful and sensitive person will feel attracted, and will be there as often and as long as possible. And the practice of the Church, which has instituted perpetual adoration, is just as clear.

~EDITH STEIN: SELF PORTRAIT IN LETTERS, P. 141

In a letter to Mother Petra Bruning, O.S.U., in Dorsten, Germany, Sister Teresa Benedicta wrote:

(SPEAKING OF THE NAME THAT CARMELITE NUNS TAKE) since all of them have an inner connection, each single one contains the entire fullness of God. Among us the Sacred Heart and the Blessed Sacrament are most frequently represented.

~*EDITH STEIN: SELF PORTRAIT IN LETTERS*, P. 188

17

Padre Valentin de San Jose

PADRE VALENTIN died in 1989 in the desert Carmel of San Jose de Batuecas (Salamanca in Spain) after a long holy life. For nearly twenty years, he lived in this holy desert. Ordained a priest on the island of Cuba in 1921, he eventually served as superior provincial of the Discalced Carmelites of Castille. Many of his writings were about the Eucharist and were read only after his death.

~*LA DIVINA EUCHARISTICA,*
PADRE VALENTIN DE SAN JOSE, O.C.D., P. 37

— ✣ —

IN THE EUCHARIST THERE IS THE SUBSTANCE, . . . and the expanse of the Body of Christ; . . . for a miracle of the Omnipotence of Jesus, is an expanse . . . .

The holy Head and the trunk, the members do not occupy the volume and dimensions which for nature ought to occupy, but that all the parts of the organism of Christ are found in all his integrity in all the Host and in each one of his smallest particles. . . . It is that the quantity of the body of Christ does not follow the laws of nature . . . but the laws of the substance, . . . for the same, all the quantity, as all the substance, in total and in each one of the consecrated species . . . .

No the Body of the Lord is subject directly to local movement, only how the body of the Redeemer is motionless in the Eucharist, like this is impassive. . . . The body of Christ has no weight, for the double reason of his remaining in glory and his remaining sacramental.

Oh Jesus! You are here on the altar, in the tabernacle, in my miserable breast Your priest has pronounced one word: and they, for these children of yours to be able and of your love, to have broken the law of equilibrium—and above all—that your thought founded the material world. And here you remain in all the loveliness of the human word, and with the poor appearance of a piece of bread: the Man-God, with you coming to your modern ones, with you come the angels in glory, certainly seen in your real presence in the sacrament.

~La Divina Eucharistica,
Padre Valentin de San Jose, O.C.D., p. 37

Jesus enriches the soul according to the humility and the love with which he is received.

Jesus instituted the Eucharist . . . to [feed] souls, . . . [to sustain] supernatural life,

18

Servant of God
Père Jacques
de Jesus Bunel

PÈRE JACQUES was born January 20, 1900, in Barentin, France. He was an altar boy, enjoyed participating in family fun, and was an excellent student as well. He placed first in his First Holy Communion class of sixty-five. He entered the minor seminary when he was only twelve, but his major seminary days were interrupted by military service in World War II.

Later, when he was ordained a priest, he was head-master of the Petite College in Avon, France. He was well loved by the students, and lived with them to be constantly available to assist them. He was arrested for harboring Jewish students among his Catholic boys during the Nazi persecution. The story of his heroic efforts was made into a movie, *Au Revoir Les Enfants* (1979).

Father Bunel was taken to the terrible prison camps of Mauthausen, Compiègne, and Fontainebleau. There, he tried to say Mass in secret, and would save scraps of bread to consecrate and share with fellow prisoners. He comforted prisoners, and even when freedom came, he insisted on being one of the last to leave. He died shortly after his release in 1945 as a result of the harsh treatment received in the camps.

— ✤ —

OUR PARTICIPATION AT MASS, our grace-filled actions, our Communions must be religious acts stamped with prayer and love. Our material work of the day must be a work bathed in prayer.

~PÈRE JACQUES RESPLENDENT IN VICTORY, P. 166

THERE IS SO MUCH I STILL HAVE TO SAY to you about Christ, especially about his Incarnation for us in the Eucharist. The Word Incarnate is always there for us in the Eucharist. This overpowering mystery allows the unworthy hands of the priest to hold the same body of Christ that the virgin Mary held in her arms and pressed to her heart. Yet it is the same Christ! The priest takes Christ in his hands and gives him to others!

When you receive him, you are like the virgin Mary during the months she carried her child. You truly carry Christ within you and want to be absorbed in profound thanksgiving. You carry him living within you! How necessary is silence so that the Holy Spirit can reveal to us the grandeur of this mystery.

~*PÈRE JACQUES RESPLENDENT IN VICTORY*, P. 168

This is the prayer he composed before his ordination to the diaconate.

O my Christ,
Communion,
Is the mystery of Your love,
Is life for souls,
Is the sure salvation for those who
Understand and receive It.
Therefore place in my mind,
Fervent and clear thoughts,
Put on my lips ardent and
Enlightening words,
That I may illumine all these souls,
That I may enkindle in them
Love for Your divine Sacrament;
And that in them, your work
Of transformation may be fulfilled.

~*1929 EUCHARISTIC CONGRESS OF HAVRE.*

PEOPLE WHO KNEW PÈRE JACQUES were impressed with his holiness. This was expressed by Xavier de V. who relates, "I was always particularly struck by Père Jacques' aspect of joyous holiness, above all at the moment of the elevation during his Mass. At such a moment, it seemed to me that he was talking with God as to a person close at hand."

~*PÈRE JACQUES*, P. 129

While in prison Père Jacques was frequently deprived of Holy Communion. He lamented, "I cannot receive Holy Communion as often as I desire, but Lord, are not you all-powerful? Dwell in me, as in the tabernacle, do not ever leave me. . . ."

~*PÈRE JACQUES*, P. 221

19

Saint Teresa of Jesus of the Andes

FEAST DAY:
July 13

CANONIZED IN 1993, SAINT TERESA OF JESUS OF THE ANDES (Juanita Fernandez Solar) is a great role model for youth. She was a beautiful, lively young woman who was born in 1900 in Santiago, Chile, and died in 1920. She entered the Carmelite convent in the Andes, following her heart's desire. But the young nun lived as a Carmelite only eleven months. She was allowed to make her religious vows after such a short time because it was clear that death was imminent.

From the time that Teresa was seven years old, she begged to receive Holy Communion. However, it wasn't until she was ten that she did. Juanita's flaming love for the Eucharist blazed out on her First Communion day. She describes it this way:

My First Communion was a cloudless day. I remember that afterward, when I went out, they put a white veil on me. In the evening, I asked for forgiveness. I remember the impression it made on my father. I went to ask his forgiveness and he kissed me. Then afterward I knelt down and, shedding tears, I begged him to pardon me for all the pains I had caused him by my conduct. And tears streamed down from my father's eyes as he picked me up and, kissing me, said there was nothing I had to beg his pardon for because I had never displeased him. He was very happy to see me be so good. Oh, yes, dear father, it was because you were so indulgent and good to me. I begged pardon of my mother, who was crying. I did the same to all my brothers and, finally, my mamita and the rest of the servants. All were deeply touched as they answered me. And, as I was on retreat, I stayed apart and so I did not eat at the family table.

The eleventh of September, 1910, the centenary year of my country, was a year of happiness and of the purest recollections I shall have in my whole life. That was a happy day for me, and a beautiful day for nature as well. The sun gave off its rays and filled my soul with happiness and thanksgiving for the Creator.

I got up early. My mother helped me put on my dress. She combed my hair. She did everything for me, but I was not thinking of anything. I was completely indifferent to everything, except to my soul for God.

When we arrived, we began praying the rosary for First Communion. Instead of the Hail Mary, we kept reciting, "Come, my Jesus, come. Oh my Savior, come yourself to prepare my heart."

The moment came. Two by two we made our entrance into the Chapel. You, my mother, were at the head of the procession and Monsignor Jara—who would give us the Sacred Communion—was at the end. We all entered with our eyes lowered, without looking at anyone. We knelt down on the kneelers that were covered with a very fine white cloth, with a white lily and a candle on each side. Monsignor Jara spoke such tender and beautiful words to us that we were all crying. I recall one thing he told us: "Ask Jesus Christ that, if you will ever commit a mortal sin, that he take you today, since your souls are as pure as the snow on the mountains. Pray to him for your parents, the authors of your existence. For those who have lost their parents, this is the moment to seek to be united with them. Yes, you are approaching to become witnesses of the legitimate union of your souls with Jesus Christ. Look at the angels of the altar, dear little girls. Look at them, they envy you. All heaven is present." I was crying. Finally he told us that he did not want to delay any further our union with Jesus because we were already hungering for him, Jesus Christ himself.

While we were approaching the altar they were singing that beautiful hymn, "Happy the Soul," which I shall never forget.

It is impossible to describe what took place between my soul and Jesus. I asked him a thousand times if he would take me, and I experienced his dear voice for the first time. "Oh Jesus I love you, I adore you!" I prayed to him for everybody. And I felt the virgin near me. Oh, how my heart expanded! For the first time I experienced a delicious peace. After we made our thanksgiving, we went to the patio to share things with the poor and each one went to embrace her family. My daddy kept kissing me and, being so happy, lifting me up in his arms. Many little girls came to the house that day.

That very happy day ended but it will be the unique day of my life. . . . Since that first embrace, Jesus did not let me go but took me for himself.

Every day, I went to Communion and talked with Jesus for a long time, but my special devotion was [to] the Virgin. I told her everything. From that day on, the earth no longer held any attraction for me. I wanted to die and I begged Jesus to take me on the eighth of December.

~GOD THE JOY OF MY LIFE, P. 113

The following letters give a hint of the love she has for Holy Communion.

To Carmen De Castro Ortuzar:

On the tenth we'll have the joy of going to the Lourdes Shrine in Santiago. I beg you to pray for me till the tenth, and also to remember to pray for me all these days when you go to Holy Communion. I assure you that I envy you with my whole soul because you can go to Holy Communion.

~*Letters of Saint Teresa of the Andes*, p. 17

She writes to Mother Angelica Teresa:

Throughout this year, except for a few days, my prayer and Communion have been like that (dry) so much. In fact, at times, I don't feel like going to Communion, because I say to myself: "Why do you think Jesus wants you to receive Him in Communion with your soul as hard as a rock?" Still, a love not felt that lives in the deepest part of my soul makes me go up to receive my Jesus. . . . I want to suffer that dryness so that other souls can feel an attraction for Communion and prayer.

~*Letters of Saint Teresa of the Andes*, p. 52

Bread of Heaven

In a letter to her sister, Rebecca, she relates:

THANK GOD, WE HAVE ALWAYS HAD MASS and we've had the Blessed Sacrament. Since Eli, Gorda, and I are the sacristans, we've spent moments of heaven by our Lord's side.

~*LETTERS OF SAINT TERESA OF THE ANDES*, P. **79**

In a letter to Father José Blanche, C.M.F., she writes:

SOON WE'LL BE GOING TO THE COUNTRY, and the only thing I don't like about it is that I won't be able to go to Communion. And without Communion I am very bad. But I'll make a spiritual Communion.

~*LETTERS OF SAINT TERESA OF THE ANDES*, P. **89**

To Father Antonio Maria Falgueras, S.J.:

FROM THE TIME OF MY FIRST HOLY COMMUNION, our Lord spoke to me after Communion and told me things I'd never suspected. And when I asked him, he would tell me things that were going to happen, and then they really did occur. But I went on thinking that everyone who went Communion was treated this way.

~*LETTERS OF SAINT TERESA OF THE ANDES*, P. **196**

In her letter to her mother, Juanita writes:

Let's take full advantage of things and thus enrich our Communion time. Let's bathe ourselves in that fount of holiness and pray for souls all over the world, because he can't say "No" to us. His heart is beating lovingly and in time with ours so that all of our desires are his, and he is all-powerful. What a wonderful identification with him! For me, those moments are heaven, with no shadow of exile. What more can I desire when God himself is already mine!

~*Letters of Saint Teresa of the Andes, p.* 261

In another letter to Father Blanche she complains:

I'm unable to go to Holy Communion here. I hunger for my Jesus.

~*Letters of Saint Teresa of the Andes, p.* 109

20

Sister Miriam of the Holy Spirit

ONE CANNOT OMIT JESSICA POWERS—such a great poet, Carmelite nun, and a mystic. Sister Miriam of the Holy Spirit was born in Wisconsin in 1905, and lived on a farm. Briefly, she attended Marquette University, majoring in journalism. This ended with her mother's illness and death.

Miriam then remained on the family farm for some years, helping her brothers until they married. She entered the Carmel of the Mother of God in Milwaukee in 1942. There she continued to write poetry, which she had begun to do while still in grammar school. Sister Miriam was a prolific writer and her poems are loved to this day.

However, in searching for some of her words on the Eucharist, it proved to be a difficult task. Most of her work covers other topics so only two will be included. Sister Miriam died in 1988, and left behind her rich legacy cherished by the sisters of Pewaukee Carmel.

— ✣ —

Prayer for Good Friday

Out of the desert of our unredemption
The Lord hath led us to a Promised Land
By the direction of His holy Hand.
Pity us, Jesus, and assist us, Mary,
For we betrayed Him at a dark command.
O Miserere.
He is the First Born for our sake bore the scourging
And led us out of our captivity
Through His own Blood, spilled out as a Red Sea.
Pity us, Jesus, and assist us, Mary,
For we imprisoned Him Who set us free.
O Miserere.
He opened up the sea of our salvation;
Pillar of cloud, His love came down to trace
A pathway for us to a lighted place.
Pity us, Jesus, and assist us, Mary,
For there was Blood and spittle on His Face.

O Miserere.
He fed us with the Manna of His making;
The Bread of Self Who yearned to be our All,
The Wine of His own Blood Which He let fall.

~*PLACE OF SPLENDOR*, JESSICA POWERS, P. **75**

The Hidden Christ

I went into the Christmas Cave;
There was no Child upon the straw.
The ox and ass were all I saw.

I sought His stable where He gave
His goodness in the guise of bread.
Emptiness filled me instead.

Filled with my Father's words, I cried
"Where have You hid Yourself?" and all
The living answered to my call.

I found Him (and the world is wide)
Dear in His warm ubiquity.
Where heart beat, there was Christ for me.

I went back to the Christmas cave,
Glad with the gain of everywhere,
And lo! The blessed Child was there.

Bread of Heaven

Then at His feasting board He gave
Embrace. He multiplied His good
And fed me in the multitude

~*SELECTED POETRY OF JESSICA POWERS,* **1963**

21

Erzsebet Szanto Kindelmann, T.O.C.

ERZSEBET WAS BORN IN HUNGARY IN 1913. She was orphaned at an early age and knew great deprivation. She only completed four years of school. After unsuccessful attempts to be admitted to four different religious orders, Erzsebet married a tradesman. He died after sixteen years of marriage, leaving Erzsebet with six children to support. She worked tirelessly to support her family, and had no time for any recreation. She did become a Third Order Carmelite, and this gave her the courage to continue with faith the hard struggle that filled her whole life.

Erzsebet had a spiritual transformation and began practicing great penances and fasts. She lived in utter poverty, and spent numerous vigils in prayer.

In 1961, Erzsebet began having deep spiritual experiences and messages from Jesus and Our Lady. These were approved by Archbishop Besnaraino Ruiz, Archbishop of Guayaquil, Ecuador, in 1988. He not only gave permission for her book to be published, but encouraged the faithful to read it. As in all private revelations, the faithful do not have to believe in them.

In 1985, Erzebet died and met Jesus whom she had longed for. Her identity had been kept secret until after her death. These words from her diary are the only passages she wrote pertaining to the Eucharist. Instead, she was given a special mission to spread devotion to the Flame of Love of the Immaculate Heart of Mary.

— ✤ —

1961

. . . I ARRANGED MY LIFE so that I could go to worship the Blessed Sacrament every day. I asked the sister who was the caretaker of the church to give me a key. After a while, with Father's permission I received the precious key. This way I had free access to the church even at night.

~*FLAME OF LOVE OF THE IMMACULATE HEART*
OF MARY, ERZSEBET SZANTO, T.O.C., P. 31

ONE DAY AS I VISITED THE BLESSED SACRAMENT, the evil one tormented me with terrible thoughts. . . . The next day my spiritual balance was restored during Holy Communion.

~*FLAME OF LOVE OF THE IMMACULATE HEART OF MARY*, ERZSEBET SZANTO, T.O.C., P. 34

JESUS: "MY CARMELITE DAUGHTER! Give yourself to me completely. It is the only way you can offer sacrifice to me. . . . I ask you for great sacrifices. Every Thursday and Friday, fast on bread and water and offer it for twelve priestly souls. On both days, spend four hours before me and make reparation for the wrong committed against me. Console me and be absorbed in my sufferings. On Friday from noon to three o'clock, worship my sacred body and blood, which was shed for the sins of the world.

"Thursday: Devote this day for atonement to the Holy Eucharist. Spend four hours in my presence. Pray with great devotion to console me for injustices against me. Absorb yourself in my agony and torturous sufferings. You'll draw abundant spiritual strength from this."

~*FLAME OF LOVE OF THE IMMACULATE HEART OF MARY*, ERZSEBET SZANTO, T.O.C., P. 38

Lament of the Lord:

... "THEN I HID MYSELF like a little child in its swaddling-clothes, in a plain little Host, to be more approachable to you and to eliminate fear."

January 2, 1963:

I WAS IMMERSED IN THE DAILY ONE-HOUR ADORATION of the Lord in the church of Mariaremete. I had prostrated myself before the Lord, telling him: "My adorable Jesus!" Suddenly I heard his grateful words:

"Tell me, tell me again, 'My adorable Jesus'! I have told you on other occasions how much this pleases me. If you could not say anything else during the whole hour you spend before me, only just say that, say it!"

~FLAME OF LOVE OF THE IMMACULATE HEART
OF MARY, ERZSEBET SZANTO, T.O.C., P. 72

February 10, 1963:

I STARTED TO SHIVER IN THE COLD CHURCH. I was ready to leave, when I heard the voice of the Lord: "Do not leave me alone! I will be alone without consolation! Oh, How many times I am alone!" Then he asked: "Tell me, since I share my house with you and you have free entrance anytime, did you see anybody with me?" I answered with my head down: "No, oh Lord, I did not meet anybody."

Pain and sorrow filled my soul. "You see, this is why you should not leave me alone. Let me give you the bounty of my graces! They are piled up in my heart's immeasurable love. Our hearts should beat together! Bring many souls to me! . . . In return, when you are lonely, I will not leave you alone either. I will be beside you in your hour of trial. Anyway, I will walk you home with the piercing look of my eyes."

~FLAME OF LOVE OF THE IMMACULATE HEART OF MARY, ERZSEBET SZANTO, T.O.C., P. 79

January, First Sunday:

I WAS IN THE HOSPITAL VISITING ONE OF MY CHILDREN. It was terribly cold. I almost could not walk. Then it came to my mind that at five o'clock the adoration of the Blessed Sacrament for the parish would start. I wanted to be there. I suppressed the feeling of cold in me and went to church. As I walked to church, the Lord Jesus started to speak: "I am very glad that you are coming to visit me. I like that you want to please me. This will mean a new flood of graces for you."

While I adored him in the Holy Eucharist, he asked me to console him for those who refuse to listen to his suggestions.

~FLAME OF LOVE OF THE IMMACULATE HEART OF MARY, ERZSEBET SZANTO, T.O.C., P. 96

January 16, 1964:

The Strength of the Precious Blood:

DURING MASS, AND AFTER HOLY COMMUNION, Jesus spoke of the power of his precious blood: "I am the blood-donor for the world. You can become intoxicated from my divine blood. Is your mind able to grasp this? It is difficult! I am the only blood-donor of the world. Meditate upon this! Try to comprehend my immeasurable love! My precious blood is warming the lame strength of your soul. I would like to pour my blood over and into all souls on earth. All that you need to do is to place yourselves completely into my divine hands. Let me do my work in your souls! Why should you remain ordinary souls? You must desire to share in my divine life—thus I can find my pleasure in you, to grow in you and with you.

"My table is ceaselessly set! I am the host and have sacrificed everything. I give myself! I, the host, sacrificed everything. I give myself to you! After receiving the precious blood, look into your souls and try to grasp the great stirrings which come through the strength of my blood. Do not be so insensitive! You should not come to my table out of habit, but urged on by the fire of love which is ignited in my Love and by me and which—together with you—burns the sins from your souls."

~*FLAME OF LOVE OF THE IMMACULATE HEART*
OF MARY, ERZSEBET SZANTO, T.O.C., PP. 97, 98

March 3, 1964:

. . . "I LET MYSELF BE KNOWN TO YOU AS GOD AND MAN. Not only you but all those who eat my body and drink my blood know this. My human heart beats together with my divinity and your human heart. Do you know what that means? It means that you become a part of my divinity. This is the portion of all those who want to feel with me, who think with me. The person who lives with me will only praise me! This praise augments the success of my work for salvation. This success will make saints of you. See, it is an eternal circulation between heaven and earth, the unending sacrifice! . . ."

~FLAME OF LOVE OF THE IMMACULATE HEART OF MARY, ERZSEBET SZANTO, T.O.C., p. 104

October 17, 1965:

WHEN THE PRIEST SAID THE WORDS of the Consecration, Jesus let me feel the wonderful transubstantiation of the host, while he said: "This is what I do for you, and for many souls. The special grace of my divine love lets you feel the magnificence of this moment in your soul."

My soul trembled from the wonder of the transubstantiation even several hours later.

~FLAME OF LOVE OF THE IMMACULATE HEART OF MARY, ERZSEBET SZANTO, T.O.C., p. 119

August 15, 1980:

OUR LADY: "PRIESTS, IF THEY FAST ON BREAD AND WATER on Mondays, will free a multitude of souls from purgatory that week at each Mass they say when the Transubstantiation takes place. Those souls consecrated to God and the faithful who keep fasting on Mondays, at the moment of Holy Communion, also will free a multitude of souls from Purgatory that week!"

OUR LADY: "If you attend holy Mass on days on which there is no obligation, the light of my Flame of Love will envelop those for whom the Mass is offered. During your participation in this Mass, the blinding of Satan will increase in proportion to your fervor."

~*FLAME OF LOVE OF THE IMMACULATE HEART*
OF MARY, ERZSEBET SZANTO, T.O.C., P. 125

22

Contemporary
Carmelites

GHISLAIN MUTETERI, O.C.D.

GHISLAIN is from the Democratic Republic of the Congo, and completed his studies for the priesthood at the seminary in Nairobi, Kenya. He was ordained a priest on May 22, 2005, in Kinshasa in Congo. A young man who is very musically inclined and joyful, he has a mother and a younger brother in the Congo. Father Ghislain enjoys playing the keyboard for liturgical celebrations and also likes to dance. He speaks six languages and actually apologizes for his English! Now assigned to a parish back in the Congo, you will see how modest he is when you read his words about the

Blessed Sacrament being the center and heart of his priesthood.

— ✤ —

Following Mary
the Ever Perfect Adorer of Christ

Awake from your slumber, O you who are still asleep! Is your heart so blind that it cannot recognize the majesty and worthiness of the Blessed Sacrament? Behold, this Holy Eucharist which we daily celebrate, this body and blood of Christ which we daily receive! Ever should we adore the Eucharist! It is the body and blood of he who once, though of divine condition, took flesh in the womb of the Blessed Virgin Mary. None, you know from among those born of women, has ever been a perfect adorer of Christ, except his holy Mother Mary. Thus, my friend, learn how to contemplate the Eucharist in deep adoration. It is the body and blood of he who was and is always contemplated and adored by Mary. Whenever you see a priest taking the blessed host from the tabernacle for adoration, try to think of Mary contemplating in a loving adoration the fruit of her womb, that little baby wrapped in swaddling clothes and held in her arms and against her chest. For indeed, Mary was the first and perfect human tabernacle of a God made man.

Moreover, Mary is the first and perfect adorer of a vulnerable, frail Son of God held at her bosom. Mary constantly was amazed at her son. Throughout Jesus' life she kept all about her son in her heart. Are not these signs and qualities of a perfect adorer! She kept on contemplating and adoring her Son until that crucial moment on the cross.

Who would not recognize, in Mary, a perfect adorer when her heart was agonized as she looked at her son hanging on a cross. She saw his crucified body all covered by blood! What could Mary have seen when she received, in her arms, the lifeless body of her son. Deep in her silent sufferings, contemplating the body of Jesus, Mary was in adoration. Surely, Mary never stopped adoring her son. Even now, she is in a perpetual adoration more perfectly in heaven where together with the angels and saints in an unending song, she is adoring the Lamb of God who is worthy of power, honor, and glory.

Therefore, my friend, place yourself under the guidance of this mother! Through your baptism, you have been incorporated into Christ. Like Mary, you have accepted the role of bearing Christ. And through the Eucharist, Christ dwells in your heart which is his living tabernacle. Why should you not fall in loving adoration of that honorable guest who has come to you so that you may become one with him! I tell you, there is no greater moment than the one of consecration of the bread and wine that become the Body and Blood of Christ during the Holy Sacrifice of the Mass! In the

Eucharistic celebration, divine mysteries are disclosed: the incarnation of the adorable Son of God, his passion and resurrection, and his second coming in glory. Following Mary's steps, let yourself continuously contemplate and adore Christ every moment that he comes to dwell in your heart. Let yourself adore him in the daily sacrifice of the Mass until he comes in glory! Amen.

Come, Let us Adore the Ever Precious Blood and Body of Christ

Encounter that unifies God and man,
Unifying Eucharist, you are adorable!
Christ, through you, O holy sacrament, ever
    present he is;
human and divine, he draws us to him,
Assuring that you and I abide in his love.
Recognizable, indeed, he is under these sacred
    species.
I and you my brother, my sister
Singing this wonderful and marvelous reality,
Tenderly and with respect come and let us adore
    him!

Most precious blood and body of Christ our Lord,
Oh heavenly banquet freely offered to us
Sanctify us from all iniquities,

To you humbly and with respect, we come in
   adoration!
Blessed and precious, truly you are!
Little, though is our faith,
Engage our mind and spirit
So that we may grow in faith and hope,
Serving you in perpetual adoration;
Everlasting presence of a loving God,
Divine presence of God made flesh.

Source and summit of our Christian life
All sweetness of life comes from you!
Cooling spring of divine grace
Recreate anew our hearts,
Attract and draw all life to a life of charity.
Most blessed sacrament of the altar
Essential spiritual food for our life
Nourish and strengthen whoever receives you,
Totally lost in your amazing majesty.

With you we rejoice and exult
Eagerly we stare at you!

Ah, arise my brother, my sister,
Delightfully, on our knees, let us fall!
Oh, let us fall in humble adoration
Remembering the glorious king, always
Encamped in the tabernacle for our good!

Yes, oh people of God, he is present,
Our Lord worthy of honor and glory
Under this form of bread and wine.

The following are quotes from two modern Carmelites excerpted from the Eucharistic Congress "Carmel and the Eucharist" in San Francisco in 1993.

BERNARD PERKINS, O.C.D.

FATHER PERKINS entered the Discalced Carmelite noviteate in California in 1958 and made his solemn profession in 1964. He was ordained a priest in 1982. He has served at the Carmelite House of Studies in Berkeley, as spiritual assistant to several O.C.D.S. communities and as superior at El Carmelo Retreat House in Redlands, California. Excerpts from his homily for the votive Mass of the Sacred Heart at the Eucharistic Congress are especially inspiring.

— ❖ —

Homily at the Votive Mass of the Sacred Heart Eucharistic Congress

TO CREATE AN INTIMATE BOND between us and himself, God in Christ willed that a sacrament be instituted to bring about a personal union between the human and the divine. This sacrament is the Holy Eucharist.

Through an encounter with Christ in the Eucharistic liturgy, which encompasses the *hearing* of sacred scripture (which the biblical Jews called "bread"), the invitation to *offer* oneself together with the gifts of bread and wine, we are then prepared for the hidden climactic change that takes place in the consecration of the bread and wine into the body and blood of Jesus. At that moment heaven, shall we say, reaches down to earth.

. . . We are then called to *reception* of Holy Communion when the living Eucharistic Christ assimilates himself with us, becoming flesh of our flesh, blood of our blood. Consequently, the mysterious union between the divine and human become a reality and we live on earth as though in heaven.

. . . Because this Eucharistic Jesus is also the risen and glorified Lord, he is not only a human presence in the heavenly kingdom, but also the fulfillment of a promise made personally to each one of us at the Last Supper, a promise by which Christ takes us to himself in the Eucharist and bestows on us the gifts of peace, charity, and unity.

. . . For Carmelites in particular, it is important that in the living out of our call and invitation to transformation, that we not only become but remain Eucharistic-centered people. This truth is supported by our history and legacy. The first Carmelites, the brethren of the prophet Elijah, erected a chapel on

Mount Carmel, so they would gather, not just weekly as was their custom, but *daily* to hear the inspired word and to receive Jesus to whom they pledged their allegiance. Through this daily Eucharistic encounter, our forefathers on Mount Carmel became more conscious of the living God in whose presence all Carmelites stand.

DR. KEITH EGAN, T.O.C.

DR. EGAN is a married Third Order Carmelite who has a bachelor's degree in philosophy, a master's in medieval history, and a doctorate in medieval religious history. He is a professor and emeritus chair of the department of Religious Studies at Saint Mary's College in Notre Dame, Indiana, and adjunct professor of theology at the University of Notre Dame. He has received many scholarly awards and honors and is widely published. This excerpt is taken from a talk at the 1993 Eucharistic Congress: "Carmel: A Eucharistic Community."

— ❖ —

. . . DISCIPLES OF JESUS HAD BEEN CELEBRATING the Eucharist in a variety of ways for centuries by the time the Carmelite hermits gathered on Mount Carmel at the Wadi-'ain-es-Siah about 1200 A.D. Since then, like other Christians, Carmelites, religious and lay, have celebrated the Eucharist in diverse ways. What is unvaried is this: the Eucharist has been at the heart of Christian and Carmelite life from the origins of Christianity and from the inception of the Carmelite Order. . . .

The Eucharist is the meal celebrated by the disciples of Jesus, a sacrificial meal that is the "Church's entire spiritual wealth," a meal that manifests the presence of the Church. Religious orders have long experimented with ways to follow Jesus, and the tension between community and solitude. The Eucharistic meal is at the center of this Carmelite tension, a place where the human and the divine encounter each other at the table of the Lord.

DISCALCED CARMELITE HERMIT

THIS LITTLE HERMIT wishes to remain anonymous, but generously contributes these words about the Eucharist.

— ✤ —

Oh, beloved
I love to sit before you here
Present in the Most Blessed Sacrament.

You pierce through the veil that separates
Us.
You penetrate my very being.

Bread of Heaven

My soul is aflame with your love,
Your healing touch,
You fill me with your love, your joy, and
Your peace.
I thirst for you, I long for you, more, my
Beloved one.

So still, in this stillness
All stops, nothing exists but you.

No time, no space.
The stillness is you, the stillness is love.

In this profound silence and solitude
I have been loved by LOVE itself.

I have found my beloved one
Keep me in the stillness of your love.

House of Bread

Oh, House of Bread,
Which feeds and nourishes my soul,
In the Eucharist I absorb you.
In death, You absorb me.
In the Eucharist, we are one.

LINDA CIESLUKOWSKI, O.C.D.S

LINDA IS A SECULAR DISCALCED CARMELITE, a member of the Community of Our Lady of Mount Carmel and Saint Joseph in Elysburg, Pennsylvania. She is the past president of the community and is a Eucharistic minister in her parish.

— ❖ —

Litany to the Holy Eucharist

Heart of Jesus in the Eucharist, sweet
Compassion of our exile, (I adore You)
Eucharistic heart of Jesus,
Heart solitary, heart humiliated,
Heart abandoned, heart forgotten,
Heart, despised, heart outraged,
Heart, ignored by men,
Heart, lover of our hearts,
Heart, pleading for our love,
Heart, patient in waiting for us,
Heart, eager to hear our prayers,
Heart, desirous that we should pray to you,
Heart, source of fresh graces,
Heart, desiring to speak to souls,

Heart, sweet refuge of the hidden life,
Heart, teacher of the secrets of union with
God,
Heart of him who sleeps, yet ever watches,
Eucharistic heart of Jesus, have mercy on me a
sinner!

DEAREST JESUS, VICTIM, I wish to comfort you. I unite myself in union with you. I count myself as nothing before you. I desire to forget myself in order to think of you. To be forgotten and despised for love of you. Not to be understood, not to be loved except by you. I will hold my peace that I may listen to you. I will forsake myself that I may lose myself in you! Dearest Jesus, please grant me the grace that I may slake your thirst for my salvation, your burning thirst for my sanctification. That being purified, I may bestow on you a pure and true love and I will no longer weary your expectations. My Jesus, take me, I beg of you! I give myself to you. I entrust to you all my actions. I give you my mind that you may enlighten it. My heart, that you may possess it. My will, that you may direct it. My misery, that you may relieve it. My soul and body, that you may nourish them.

Dearest Eucharistic heart of my king, whom I love and whose blood is the life of my soul. May it no longer be I that live, but you who live in me! Amen.

23

Luis Arostegui Gamboa, O.C.D.

Father General of the Discalced Carmelite Order

FATHER LUIS AROSTEGUI GAMBOA was born in Gatica, Spain, in 1939. He was preparing for priesthood even in high school. He was professed as a Discalced Carmelite in 1956, and ordained a priest in 1964. He holds a licentiate in theology.

Father's travels have taken him from Panama to Dallas, Texas, to Milan, Italy, to Austria, Monte Carlo, back to Pamplona in Spain, and then to Guatemala, Peru, and Chile in Latin America.

He served as provincial councilor for two terms, and has taught and written many articles. Father has tirelessly shared his talents in many capacities. He gave a wonderful conference to those at the Chicago

Carmelite Studies Institute Congress. It enabled the participants to realize what a vast global community Carmel encompasses.

— ✛ —

The Eucharist, Sacrament of the Kingdom

1. Jesus has lived a dual experience: his own experience of the Father and the experience of the kingdom of God already in the world. The first is his union with the Father, which suggests itself in his prayer, often [said] in solitude (Mt 14:23; Mk 1:35; Lk 5:16), even "all night" (Lk 6:12) long. The kingdom means that the "justice" of the Father becomes reality in the world. "Justice" is equivalent to the "will" of the Father. It is his experience of the Father that Jesus wishes to communicate to all, that all enter this same relationship of confidence and affection that he lives, and simultaneously, that this "justice" saturates, inspires, and determines all the relations of men and women with each other. For Jesus, the experience of the Father and that of the kingdom are not only inseparable, but in a certain way, one and the same.

2. This new life in the kingdom of God is presented as a banquet (Mt 8:11) or a celebration (Mt 25:21–23). "Happy the one who eats in the Kingdom of God!" one exclaimed (Lk 14:15). It is the banquet to which

he invites you and all classes of people until the house is filled (Lk 14:16–23; see also Mt 22:1–10). Among the occasions that show that the kingdom of God has arrived is the one in which Jesus eats with publicans and sinners (Mt 9:11) to whom this act signified closeness, acceptance, and communion. There, Jesus lives like someone present and real, like someone who teaches with parables (Lk 15).

3. In the Last Supper, Jesus, when instituting the Eucharist, interprets his death (and his life, and what is to follow) as the new covenant (Lk 22:20; 1 Cor 11:25). The new covenant is characterized as the Spirit granted to all men (Acts 2:16–18), the internal law (Heb 8:10), the experience of God (Heb 8:11; Jn 6:45; 14:23; 1 Jn 2:20–21), the pardon of sins (Heb 8:12), and universal brotherhood (Rv 4:9–10; Eph 2:13–16). That is to say, the new covenant is the kingdom of God that Jesus began to proclaim from the beginning and showed with his works and with all his being.

Jesus said: Take and eat; this is my body, which I deliver for you. Take and drink all; this is the cup of my blood, of the new and everlasting covenant, that will be shed for you and for all. "I say to you that I will not return to eat it, the Paschal Meal, (the Pascal Victim speaking) until it reaches its fulfillment in the Kingdom of God" (Lk 22:16). "I say to you that in the future I will not drink of this fruit of the vine until the day that I drink it with you in the Kingdom of my Father" (Mt 26:29). "I entrust the Kingdom to

you as my Father entrusted it to me: so that you eat
and drink and seat yourselves in twelve thrones to
govern the twelve tribes of Israel" (Lk 22:30). Here,
we have the eating and drinking of the aforesaid
Eucharist at the table of the kingdom.

4. In the Last Supper, there are two lines that explain
to us that the kingdom is for those who live and die
in Jesus. At the same time, they explain what he is
doing and saying in the Supper (and what the
Eucharist is). 1. "I am in the midst of you who
serve" (Lk 22:24–27). 2. The washing of the feet. The
Gospel of John does not relate to the institution of
the Eucharist but includes the episode of the washing of the feet (Jn 13:1–17). In the discourse that fol-
lows appears the commandment of this kingdom,
whose sacrament is the Eucharist: "This is my commandment: that you love others as I have loved
you" (Jn 15:12–17).

Jesus is in the center, delivering himself for the
kingdom. He gives himself as a servant who wash-
es their feet, and says, "Love one another as I have
loved you." He gives himself until his death on the
cross. When in church, we say "do this in memory
of me," "this" means all that Jesus does and is. This
includes the Last Supper, the supper of the kingdom which represents the celebration of all people
called to the kingdom of justice and brotherhood,
and to the kingdom of the Beatitudes and the
Magnificat. Those who eat this meal in unity with
the Lord announce the kingdom of justice and the

sanctity of God "all in all." They exemplify the truth of the Eucharist which is the kingdom.

Jesus sits at the center among his companions at the table. He is the one to be delivered for sacrifice but he sits surrounded by his disciples, celebrating the banquet of the kingdom. Like the favorite disciple John, each one of them longs to be very close to Jesus (Jn 13:23–25). Happily, the Eucharist offers the most personal relationship with Jesus. "I live with faith in the Son of God, who loved me and was given up for me" (Gal 2:20). Simultaneously, that proximity to Christ is vital in the celebration of the Feast of the Kingdom.

5. That the elements of the Eucharist are bread and wine does not represent a miracle or a wonderful caprice of God. They are the normal elements of festive food. It is also appropriate that the food represents the banquet of the kingdom, the food of reconciliation with the Father (Lk 15:23) and with each other. It is the supreme sacrament because it represents the last and surrendering of Jesus for the kingdom ("there is no greater love . . ."). This food is "the real presence" because the sacrament of the kingdom really shows that no one else is Jesus; it presents the truth of Jesus. The sacrifice of the cross is present at this meal because Jesus gives himself now like then. He is the one that is eternally given.

6. The miracle that is the basis for all of this is that Jesus is Jesus. He is the Son of God who loves us

and gave himself for us. He lives in us, with us, among us. . . . The second miracle is that "the Kingdom comes."

24

Pope John Paul II

THE PERFECT ENDING TO THIS BOOK must include some words of our Late Holy Father, Pope John Paul II. He was a Carmelite at heart. As a young man, Karol Wojtyla desired to enter a Carmelite monastery but was encouraged to become a diocesan priest instead by his bishop. Nonetheless, Father Wojtyla faithfully wore his Carmelite scapular, had deep devotion to Our Lady, and was a contemplative. As pope, this man elevated many Carmelites to be "Blessed" or "Saint," and even named Saint Thérèse of Lisieux a Doctor of the Church. There is so much that could be said about this "Carmelite connection" with Pope John Paul II. But the biography of this great pope is well known and there would not be enough space to properly treat it.

Pope John Paul II wrote much on the Eucharist, and his 2003 Encyclical Letter *Ecclesia de Eucharistia* (On the Eucharist in Its Relationship to the Church), and Mane Nobiscum Domine (Remain with Us Lord), released for the Year of the Eucharist (October 2003—October 2004) especially speak of this love of our Lord in the Eucharist.

The Encyclical Letter, Ecclesia de Eucharistia, is so rich that it would be wonderful to include it in its totality. But some carefully chosen excerpts are offered instead.

The church draws her life from the Eucharist, the pope said on many different occasions. The Second Vatican Council rightly proclaimed that the Eucharistic sacrifice is "the source and summit of the Christian life." "For the most holy Eucharist contains the Church's entire spiritual wealth: Christ himself, our passover and living bread. Through his own flesh, now made living and life-giving by the Holy Spirit, he offers life to men."

The Holy Father wrote a letter to all priests each year on Holy Thursday. But in 2003, he wished to include all of the Church in this letter. He also wanted to thank God for the gift of the Eucharist and the priesthood.

In the letter, he recalled all of the places that he has celebrated Holy Mass: "I remember the parish church of Niegowic, where I had my first pastoral assignment, the collegiate church of Saint Florian in Krakow, Wawel Cathedral, Saint Peter's Basilica, and so many basilicas and churches in Rome and throughout the world. I have been able to celebrate Holy Mass in chapels built along mountain paths, on lakeshores and seacoasts; I have celebrated it on altars built in stadiums and in city squares. . . . This varied scenario of celebrations of the Eucharist has given me a powerful experience of its universal and, so to speak, cosmic character. Yes, cosmic! Because even when it is celebrated on the humble altar of a country church, the Eucharist is always in some way celebrated on the altar of the world. It unites heaven and earth. It embraces and permeates all creation."

He wrote: "Those who feed on Christ in the Eucharist need not wait until the hereafter to receive eternal life: *They already possess it on earth,* as the first-fruits of a future fullness which will embrace man in his totality."

— ✤ —

55. In a certain sense Mary lived her *Eucharistic faith* even before the institution of the Eucharist, by the very fact *that she offered her virginal womb for the Incarnation of God's Word.* The Eucharist, while commemorating the passion and resurrection, is also in continuity with the incarnation.

Allow me, dear brothers and sisters, to share with deep emotion, as a means of accompanying and strengthening your faith, my own testimony of faith in the Most Holy Eucharist. . . . Here is the church's

treasure, the heart of the world, the pledge of the fulfillment for which each man and woman, even uncon-
sciously, yearns.

62. Let us take our place, dear brothers and sisters, *at
the school of the saints*, who are the great interpreters of
true Eucharistic piety. In them the theology of the
Eucharist takes on all the splendor of a lived reality; it
becomes "contagious" and, in a manner of speaking, it
"warms our hearts." Above all, let us *listen to Mary
Most Holy*, in whom the mystery of the Eucharist
appears, more than in anyone else, as a *mystery of light*.
Gazing upon Mary, we come to know *the transforming
power present in the Eucharist*. In her we see the world
renewed in love.

In the humble signs of bread and wine, changed
into his body and blood, Christ walks beside us as our
strength and our food for the journey, and he enables
us to become, for everyone, witnesses of hope. If, in the
presence of this mystery, reason experiences its limits,
the heart, enlightened by the grace of the Holy Spirit,
clearly sees the response that is demanded, and bows
low in adoration and unbounded love.

~*Ecclesia de Eucharista*

*For the Year of the Eucharist (October 2004–October 2005), Pope John
Paul II again wrote a jewel in honor of the Holy Eucharist, Mane Nobis
cum Domine. In this letter, he used the theme of the disciples on the way to
Emmaus throughout. These are some of his reflections.*

III
The Eucharist:
Source and Manifestation of Communion

"ABIDE IN ME, AND I IN YOU" (Jn 15:4).

19. When the disciples on the way to Emmaus asked Jesus to stay "with" them, he responded by giving them a much greater gift: through the Sacrament of the Eucharist he found a way to stay "in" them. Receiving the Eucharist means entering into a profound communion with Jesus. "Abide in me, and I in you" (Jn 15:4). This relationship of profound and mutual "abiding" enables us to have a certain foretaste of heaven on earth. Is this not the greatest of human yearnings? . . . Eucharistic communion was given so that we might be "sated" with God here on earth, in expectation of our complete fulfillment in heaven.

30. . . . . *Consecrated men and women,* called by that very consecration to more prolonged contemplation: never forget that Jesus in the tabernacle wants you to be at his side, so that he can fill your hearts with the experience of his friendship, which alone gives meaning and fulfillment to your lives. . .

31. We have before us the example of the saints, who in the Eucharist found nourishment on their journey toward perfection. How many times did they shed tears of profound emotion in the presence of this great mystery, or experience hours of inexpressible

"spousal" joy before the sacrament of the altar! May we be helped above all by the Blessed Virgin Mary, whose whole life incarnated the meaning of the Eucharist. "The Church, which looks to Mary as a model, is also called to imitate her in her relationship with this most holy mystery." The Eucharistic Bread which we receive is the spotless flesh of her Son: *Ave verum corpus natum de Maria Virgine.* In this Year of grace, sustained by Mary, may the Church discover new enthusiasm for her mission and come to acknowledge ever more fully that the Eucharist is the source and summit of her entire life.

~*MANE NOBISIUM DOMINE,* **7 OCTOBER, 2004**

Bibliography

Austrian Province of the Teresian Carmel. *Introduction to the Works of St John of the Cross- A Portrait of the Saint.* Washington, D.C. ICS Publications.

Brunot, Amedee, S.C.J. *Mariam the Little Arab.* Sister Mary of Jesus Crucified. Carmel of Maria Regina. Eugene. 1981.

Carmelite Generalate. *Constitutions of the Secular Order of Our Lady of Mount Carmel and Saint Teresa of Jesus.* Rome. 2003.

Carmelite Monastery Wheeling. *Blessed John Soreth of the Order of Carmel.* Wheeling.

Carmelo Mezzasalma e Alessandro Andreini. *Colloqui Eucharistici. Madre Maria Candida Dell'Eucharistia.* Rome. Edizioni O.C.D. 2004.

Carrouges, Michel. *Père Jacques.* New York. The MacMillan Company. 1961.

Centala, Theodore, O.C.D. *Carmelite Rule of St Albert, Secular Order Rule of Life, National Statutes of USA, Ritual for Promises and Vows.* Washington, D.C. Discalced Carmelite Friars.

Clarke, John, O.C.D. *Story of a Soul.* Washington, D.C. ICS Publications. 1972.

De La Vierge, Victor, O.C.D. *Spiritual Realism of St Thérèse of Lisieux.* Milwaukee. Bruce Publishing Company. 1961.

De Meester, Conrad, O.C.D. *Light Love Life.* Washington, D.C. ICS Publications. 1987.

Dolan, Albert H., O.Carm. *Marie: Sister of Saint Thérèse.* (Written by Pauline). Chicago. Carmelite Press.

Egan, Keith, Dr., T.O.C. *Carmel: A Eucharistic Community.* San Francisco. Congress: Carmel and the Eucharist. 1993.

Fabrini, Placido. *The Life of Saint Mary Magdalen De-Pazzi. Part I.* Philadelphia. Rev. Antonio Isoleri. 1900.

Giordano, Silvano, OCD. *Carmel in the Holy Land.* Arenzano, Italy: Messagero di Jesus Bambino di Praga. 1995. Distributed by ICS Publications. Washington, D.C.

Griffin, Michael, O.C.D. *God the Joy of my Life.* Hubertus. Teresian Charism Press. 1989.

Griffin, Michael, O.C.D. *Letters of Saint Teresa of the Andes.* Hubertus. Teresian Charism Press. 1994.

Husslein, Joseph, S.J. *The Little Flower and the Blessed Sacrament.* New York. Benziger Brothers. 1925.

John Paul II, Pope. *Ecclesia de Eucharistia.* On the Eucharist in its relationship to the Church. Boston. Pauline Books and Media. 2003.

John Paul II, Pope. *Mane Nobis Domine.* Apostolic Letter of the Holy Father to the Bishops, Clergy and Faithful for the Year of the Eucharist. The Vatican. 2004.

Kane, Aletheia, O.C.D. *The Complete Works of Elizabeth of the Trinity.* Vol.1. Washington DC. ICS Publications. 1984.

Kane, Aletheia, O.C.D. *The Prayers of Saint Thérèse of Lisieux.* Washington, D.C. ICS Publications. 1997.

Kavanaugh, Kieran, O.C.D. and Otilio Rodriguez, O.C.D. *The Collected Works of Saint Teresa of Avila.* Vol. 1. Washington, D.C. ICS. 1976.

Kavanaugh, Kieran, O.C.D. and Otilio Rodriguez, O.C.D. *The Collected Works of St Teresa of Avila.* Vol. 2. Washington, D.C. ICS Publications. 1980.

Kavanaugh, Kieran, O.C.D. and Otilio Rodriguez, O.C.D. *The Collected Works of St Teresa of Avila.* Vol. 3. Washington, D.C. ICS Publications. 1985.

Kavanaugh, Kieran, O.C.D. *The Life, Times, and Teaching of Saint John of the Cross.* Washington, D.C. ICS Publications. 2000.

Kinney, Donald, O.C.D. *Saint Thérèse Of Lisieux: Her Last Conversations.* Washington, D.C. ICS Publications. 1977.

Kinney, Donald, O.C.D. *The Poetry of Saint Thérèse of Lisieux.* Washington, D.C. ICS Publications. 1996

Koeppel, Josephine, O.C.D. *Edith Stein: Self Portrait in Letters.* Washington, D.C. ICS Publications. 1993.

Lipski, Alexander, O.C.D.S. *Bl. Elizabeth of the Trinity: The Eucharistic Victim.* Congress: Carmel and the Eucharist. San Francisco. 1993.

Murphy, Francis, S.J. *Père Jacques: Resplendent in Victory.* Washington, D.C. ICS Publications. 1998.

Nash, Ann Englund. *Elizabeth of the Trinity. The Complete Works.* Vol. II. Washington, D.C. ICS Publications. 1995.

O'Neill, George, S.J. *Blessed Mary of the Angels.* London, EC. R&T Washbourne, LTD. 1909.

Pausback, Gabriel, O.Carm. *The Complete Works of Saint Mary Magdalen De'Pazzi.* Volume I. 1969.

Perkins, Bernard, O.C.D. *Homily for the Votive Mass of the Sacred Heart.* Congress: Carmel and the Eucharist. San Francisco. 1993.

Phelim, Monahan, O.C.D. *Edith Stein in Her Writings.* Galway. Carmelite Publishing. 1998.

Powers, Jessica, O.C.D. *The Place of Splendor.* New York. Cosmopolitan Science and Art Service Co., Inc. 1946.

Rowe, Margaret. *God is Love. Saint Teresa Margaret: Her Life.* Washington, D.C. ICS Publications. 2003.

Ruiz, Federico, OCD. *God Speaks in the Night. The Life, Times and Teaching of St John of the Cross.* Washington, D.C. ICS Publications. 2000.

Siegfried, Regina, and Rev. Robert Morneau, D.D. *Selected Poetry of Jessica Powers,* Kansas City. 1989

Sugrue, Patrick, O.C.D. Carmelite Home Page. 2003.

Sullivan, John, O.C.D. *Edith Stein Essential Writings.* New York. Orbis Books. 2002.

Szanto, Erzsebet, T.O.C. *Flame of Love of the Immaculate Heart of Mary.* Edited by Stephen Foglein, M.S. Orangeville, Ca. Two Hearts Publishing Company. 1991.

Therese of St Augustine, OCD, Ven. Princess Louise of France. *Meditations Eucharistiques.*

Tierney, Tadgh, O.C.D. *The Story of Hermann Cohen, O.C.D.* Hubertus. Teresian Press. 1994.

Valabek, Redemptus, O.Carm. *Essays on Titus Brandsma Carmelite Educator Journalist Martyr.* CWP. 1985.

Valabek, Redemptus, O.Carm. *The Beatification of Father Titus Brandsma, Carmelite.* Rome. Institutum Carmelitanum. 1986.

Valentin de San Jose, O.C.D. *La Divina Eucharistica.* Batuecas. Desert of San Jose. 1990.

PENNY HICKEY, O.C.D.S., has been a secular Carmelite since 1991. Her love for the Eucharist blossomed through her work as an Extraordinary Minister of Communion in her parish and to the sick, a role she has been active in since 1981. She serves as the Formation Director for the Community of Our Lady of Mt. Carmel in Washington, D.C. She began working on this compilation of Eucharistic prayers and meditations in anticipation of the Year of the Eucharist (October 2004–October 2005).

Penny Hickey is also the author/editor of two previous books: *Behold the Lamb of God: Communion Prayers for the Sick* (Witness Ministries) and *Drink of the Stream: Prayers of Carmelites* (Ignatius Press).

She is a registered nurse who volunteers part-time as a nurse for the Mission of Mercy.

A native of New York, she and her husband John, Col., U.S. Army, Ret., live in Boiling Springs, Pennsylvania. They have four children and seven grandchildren.

Spiritual Classics

The Gospels for Prayer
Michael Hansen, S.J., Editor
Experience the profound presence of Jesus in the Gospels with this unique resource, designed especially for prayer, rather than for study. The text of the Gospels stands alone, a foundation for personal reflection and prayer; the introduction describes ten ways to pray the gospels; and the index makes it easy to find your favorite passages.
ISBN: 0-87793-986-1 / 736 pages, leather / $21.95 / Ave Maria Press

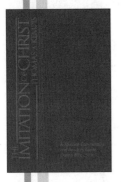

The Imitation of Christ—Thomas À Kempis
A Timeless Classic for Contemporary Readers
William C. Creasy
Working from the 1441 Latin Autograph Manuscript, Creasy succeeds in creating a different interpretation of the *Imitation* by working through its historical, cultural, and linguistic contexts. Offers profound insights into a person's relationship with God.
ISBN: 0-87061-231-X / 192 pages / $12.95 / Christian Classics

This Tremendous Lover
M. Eugene Boylan
For forty years Catholic Christians have been turning and returning to this spiritual classic, in which a Trappist monk speaks clearly and perceptively to the priest, religious, or layperson still "in the world."
ISBN: 0-87061-138-0 / 376 pages / $12.95 / Christian Classics

Available from your local bookstore or from **ave maria press**
Notre Dame, IN 46556 / www.avemariapress.com
ph: 1.800.282.1865 / fax: 1.800.282.5681
Prices and availability subject to change.

Keycode: FØTØ5Ø6ØØØØ